SHANE MACGOWAN

Bruce G Dearing

TABLE OF CONTENTS

CHAPTER 1

SHANE O'HOOLIGAN

CHAPTER 2

KING OF THE BOP

CHAPTER 3

FAREWELL TO NEW YORK CITY BOYS

CHAPTER 4

LONESOME HIGHWAY

CHAPTER 5

WANDRIN' STAR

CHAPTER 6

A FURIOUS DEVOTION

CHAPTER 1

SHANE O'HOOLIGAN

Shane was already an adolescent infatuated with pop music. As Britain spent its last pounds, shillings, and pence before decimalisation in 1971, and The Troubles in Northern Ireland spiralled out of control, Cream, Black Sabbath, Creedence Clearwater Revival, The Rolling Stones, Pink Floyd, and other bands thundered from his eerily lit bedroom, competing with the daily soundtrack of construction work outside. 'He got into music big-time at the Barbican, and he'd have albums playing all day in his room,' Maurice recalls. 'The big one was Bob Dylan, and that's when I started liking Bob Dylan. I was a real square, pretending to be literary, and I grew to love and still love Bob Dylan. I've grown to appreciate all of that rock music, especially when paired with country. My thoughts were expanding. Siobhan was right next door, watching the people enter the den. The music emanating from there was earth-shattering.'

'We had a Black Sabbath poster in the toilet,' Siobhan recalls. 'Because Mum and Dad were like that, we spread the culture throughout the house. Shane used to play his albums all day and all night, study Sounds, NME, Melody Maker, and a lot of his hippie pals were always around the flat.' Willoughby House was a terraced building in the Barbican, a complex viewed as being on the cutting edge of modern living. It was a long way from Tunbridge Wells and a world away from The Commons. The brutalist-style flats were erected on the site of a Roman watchtower, which appealed to Maurice's love of urban areas and his interest in history. It also offered a much shorter drive to his Marble Arch workplace and more chances for a post-work pint. It was edgy and cool for Shane. He describes the location as "right next to the East End." 'Some of the flats there didn't require a lot of money. The caretaker had a free flat and was paid by folks at the top of the tree. Although they didn't make a big show about it, there were people like Roger Moore and Kenny Everett in there, as well as a few pretty famous crooks.' The Barbican had been built mostly in the 1960s, but the three now-iconic tower blocks were still under construction when Shane and his family arrived. The last of them wasn't finished until 1976, so as the four of them tried to adjust to their new surroundings, there was a constant cacophony of construction work all around them. 'You'd be inside your flat, and you could shut it down if you wanted,' Shane explains. 'But me and my grandfather preferred to leave the side window open so we could hear all the commotion, the mixers and the scaffolding, and the walls being knocked down.'Stairs and another set of stairs going to the main bedroom were particularly showy. I and Siobhan each had a room, and there was a kitchen and a waste disposal device that stank the house up. Everything you placed in it chewed away, cabbage and decaying food. There was no natural light; instead, strip lighting was used. I was given a green signal. I was extremely trippy. I was on the verge of psychedelia. I lived next door to Jim Morrison when he died. He'd show up from time to time in my feverish imagination. It was a terrific place to play The Doors, and I must admit it was quite loud.' Shane had to adjust not only to what he viewed as a 'space-age' setting, but also to his new school, Westminster. His passion for books and natural ability for writing had gained him a partial scholarship at one of the country's oldest and most prestigious universities. According to the Record of Old Westminsters, he started at the school as a dayboy in January 1972, when he entered Ashburnham House. The Westminster Abbey School dates from the early fourteenth century and is located on the grounds of Westminster Abbey. Six British prime ministers attended, as well as poets, philosophers, authors, high court justices, physicists, and other notables. Among others who have graduated include former deputy prime minister Nick Clegg, actresses Helena Bonham Carter and Imogen Stubbs, actor and director John Gielgud, broadcaster Louis Theroux, and playwright Stephen Poliakoff. Shane is joined on the list of singers and musicians who travelled there by Thomas Dolby, Dido, and Mika. The solidly conservative Westminster, on the other hand, was entirely inappropriate for a teenager who was already dabbling with drugs and drawn to the seedier side of life. 'They were such wankers,' Shane says of Westminster. 'I didn't want to go,' said Holmewood. It helped me, and he [Bairamian] liked the concept of a "foreigner" attending an English gentleman's school.' Shane describes his initial thoughts as 'to stay out of the classes for as long as I can, tsscc, and I'm absolutely not doing any sports because they didn't do football. They exclusively went boating, which they called "water." We rode the train to Grove Park, which is located near Bromley. I wasn't interested at first, but after trying on one of the clothes, I realised they were great. I looked like the guy from The Yardbirds with my hair that long.' The move was doomed to fail from the outset. Shane was completely immersed in his hippy phase when he went through the doors of Westminster that winter. He was 14 years old at the time, with shoulder-length hair and a diet consisting of bananas and beans. Although he tried to fit in with his wide knowledge of music, his sole actual concentration was the music he was listening to and the records he was buying. 'I imagine he tried to listen to what the other Westminster kids were listening to at the time - Yes, Genesis, Pink Floyd, ELP, The Allman Brothers - because there was a lot of analysis of them,' says Thomas Dolby (real name Robertson), one of his classmates. But you could tell he wasn't particularly enthused about it.' His desire to be welcomed was impeded by the fact that he stuck out in terms of appearance and tone like a sore thumb. In The Pogues, he'd make a point of his strangeness, his taxi-door ears and decaying teeth. As a rake-thin teenager in the most English of schools, he was self-conscious. 'He felt hesitant, a little embarrassed about his accent and teeth, and didn't seem to fit in,' adds Thomas. 'However, he was clearly extremely brilliant.'

Shane's penchant for pranks ensured that he drew even more attention to himself. He cautioned Thomas that if they arrived in drag and were transported to the Mendip Hills for orienteering, the personnel would force them to stay on the bus and they would get off. Thomas eventually caved, and Shane ended up leading some of the others to a pub where they were discovered late at night. Shane never passed up an opportunity to crack a joke in class. 'He and I were whispering in the back row of Mr [Alan] Howarth's English class,' Thomas recalls. Shane had read the books but did not participate in the discussions. Mr Howarth, who later became a cabinet minister under Margaret Thatcher, was talking about Emily Bront or something and planned to embarrass us one day. So he inquired as to what figure of speech a certain term was. I wasn't paying attention. Shane leaned down and gently stated, "It's onanism." That's just what I stated! "Robertson, come to the front of the class and look up 'onanism' in my dictionary, and read it out loud, please." It turned out to be masturbation or ejaculating outside of the vagina, therefore I was mocked. Given Shane's history and Howarth's reputation as a jerk, it took me a few years to appreciate the irony of the joke.' Shane made certain that others would never forget him outside of the classroom. He was part of a gang that held 'inquisitions' on other students, and he was in charge of making them talk. 'If they needed information from someone, they sat next to them and I handled the interrogation, and I might have thrown a smoke or two in his face, tsscc,' he adds. 'You could squeeze his nipples and rub nettles into his pants till he screamed. And there are no dock leaves nearby to relieve it immediately, but they wouldn't have relieved this! You've got two guys preventing him from fleeing in any direction but backwards, which is a terrible idea. You simply leap on his face a few times and constantly kick him in the balls. We just gave it cool names like Minister for Torture. If they wanted me to give my all, they had to make me Minister of Torture, tsscchh.'

Despite Shane's celebrity, Westminster was accepting of students who were unusual, as long as they were bright, according to Thomas Dolby: 'Shane was seen as a troublemaker. He had horribly yellowed fingers and teeth, which the teachers were quick to point out. However, in terms of public schools, Westminster was rather liberal. They were more tolerant of different strokes, and Shane was a scholar, and scholars were admired for being extremely intelligent while coming from less privileged homes.' Shane was, without a doubt, a superb writer, continuing to compose works that were much beyond his years in terms of style and subject matter. It wasn't just his talent that made his writings, and subsequently his songs, so vivid; it was also his appreciation for quirky personalities and horrible stories. He revelled in life's ugliness and soaked up details for use in his fiction. Ted Craven, his house master at Westminster who taught English and history, looked to many of his students to be monotonous, rambling on and on about his days in the Royal Navy. Shane, on the other hand, saw it as a rich vein of material that he could mine. He heard something they didn't hear in his teacher's babbling. 'He'd go into graphic descriptions of degrees of seasickness: before the bile starts coming out, and different colours of bile, and you just had to urge him to keep talking, and the session was finished before you realised it,' says one student. Shane recalls his teacher's stories. 'And you've got a lot of detail. He really helped me out with my songs. It was like Coleridge's "The Rime of the

Ancient Mariner," except he was on a Second World War ship. You start with green bile, which is unpleasant, then blue bile, and finally black bile. That stuff would be fantastic poured into glasses and served as absinthe in a West End club.' Shane spends most of his time at home listening to music and researching his favourite bands and artists. A green light bulb hung from the ceiling, casting an odd glow on his chamber, as he sat at his desk, meticulously cutting out items from the music press. His vast record collection was housed in a large bookcase, and Siobhan would sneak in and play them when he was away. He watched Top of the Pops every week and was well-versed in the British mainstream music industry, but by reading the music press, he was exposed to the alternative culture in the United States and its punk prototypes. His evangelism for these unknown American bands astounded his prog-loving peers at Westminster. 'We used to sneak out to a coffee shop in Victoria and spend most afternoons nursing a single cup of tea and talking about music,' Thomas recalls. Shane was constantly around, smoking Woodbines. We admired his musical acumen, and he was constantly up to date on album cover trivia and lyrics. Shane came in one day, right in the thick of a heated debate on Soft Machine III [Third] or something. "It's all crap!" he exclaimed. "All that progressive rock bullshit." We were all taken aback. "Even the Beatles and the Stones - they're just a bunch of old tossers." We were stunned - this was sacrilege. "Well, what should we be listening to, Shane?" He mentioned a slew of bands we'd never heard of. "The Stooges and Iggy." The MC5. "Jonathan Thunders." Our collective fury was identical to that of the mainstream music press when the Sex Pistols appeared on the scene a year or so later.'

At Westminster, Shane wasn't simply broadening his psychedelic horizons. He was part of a tiny drug distribution network that took orders from other students and their friends and sourced them from dodgy persons in the West End, some of whom, according to Shane, were Charlie Kray allies. One of their regular sources was a doorman at a rock venue frequented by Shane.

'I was hanging around with the other guys in the drug-dealing ring. We confined it within the school or friends of people in the school because it was a tiny organisation with a lot of clients. But they could come and buy a lot, and we knew they were selling to people we'd never met, and the school had figured that out. Before I arrived, they had already gotten rid of the former head of the racket. As a result, I was approached right away to replace him as one of the point men.' Although first-year students were among their customers, Shane claims that the more exotic' shopping lists came from students higher up the school who wanted 'heroin, cocaine, LSD, mescaline, Nepalese temple balls, and things like that. They became loyal clients, and I made friends with them.' His adolescent workforce was also stealing on the job, charging 'commission' for beer, records, and other shoplifted products. Then they'd dash down to Petticoat Lane Market in the East End with their ill-gotten gains and stock up on the coveted garments and shoes they couldn't afford to buy in the stylish shops uptown. 'It was all freaking hot, so you could get it for almost nothing,' Shane explains. 'I acquired a fantastic, stunning pair of genuine winklepickers for £5.'

Westminster was already aware of his drug-dealing in school, and his court appearance heightened the situation. So, barely fourteen months after starting at the school, Shane and his father were invited to see Dr John Rae, the headmaster. 'I always remember the meeting being on a Good Friday; we often laughed about that,' Maurice says. The headmaster's name was Dr Rae, and he was a guy similar to Jacob Rees-Mogg, or Smog as we know him. He rambled on about Shane's transgressions: he'd been up to mischief at school, as well as a court appearance for smoking pot in the Barbican. Rae said he couldn't possible keep Shane in the school, which thrilled me because I knew Shane didn't need whatsoever they had to teach him; it was all within him. We knew he wasn't going to take the traditional way, therefore he didn't need any certificates; he had no academic ambitions at all. His command of the English language was so strong that he couldn't be taught; instead, he'd be teaching others. I can't recall my precise comments, but I think I thought the headmaster was a little too dignified for me to start hurling the F-word around. I was probably afraid he'd pass out. But I know I was adamant about not allowing him to attend that bloody, maybe "fucking" school. Anyway, I told him to shove it, and the meeting ended abruptly.' Shane recalls his abrupt departure from Westminster, saying, 'My mother wasn't surprised I got tossed out. We'd predicted it. My father and I were both relieved. I was with him in a meeting with Rae, and he made a remark about Ray being a racist jerk. Rae had been on my back since the beginning because I was Irish. He was attempting to return it to its former glory, when the school motto was that it produced English gentlemen. "I'm Irish, and I want to be an Irish gentleman," I used to say, and they might have laughed or not. However, the other youngsters would laugh.' Shane's expulsion may not have bothered Maurice and Shane, but it did little to calm the tempest at home. Therese had never gotten used to living on the fifth floor, and the Barbican's sombre, depressing atmosphere was affecting her health. According to Siobhan, Therese had always been apprehensive about the relocation, but she hadn't protested it because she didn't know what she thought about it. She began to experience anxiety and despair very immediately after they arrived. 'She wanted to leave London as soon as we arrived,' Maurice recalls. 'Therese was raised in rural Ireland, and living in a flat with no yard, little fresh air, or natural light made her feel claustrophobic and miserable. She sought medical attention and was prescribed Valium, which relieved her symptoms but did nothing to alleviate her depression. After much deliberation, she began seeing a psychiatrist, who prescribed Marplan, an antidepressant.' Despite her declining mental health, Therese helped Shane secure a job at the local supermarket when he was kicked out of Westminster. So, while she was in bed on depression medication, he was stacking shelves and unloading delivery trucks. 'It was a family supermarket, and they hired young people, mostly lads, who were well underage and had money in their hands,' he says. 'The dark economy is beneficial to everyone. It was sometimes strenuous work, but it was largely tedious shelf-stacking.

But every time a lorry arrived, there were giant crates holding large family tins of beans and other goodies, and around Christmas, they put out jars of gherkins and they went like the clappers. At the time, ten pounds a week was a very nice pay.' His grocery employment was to be the first of several temporary occupations he would take. Despite his unceremonious exit from Westminster, Shane wasn't finished with education. He applied to Kingsway College in Camden, which Simon John Ritchie attended before becoming Sid Vicious in the Sex Pistols. But they turned him down, ostensibly on 'ethnic grounds,' and he wound up in Hammersmith College of Further Education, which he describes as "bottom of the heap."

Shane explains, "I was doing English language and literature, history, and French." 'On the rare instances when I showed up to class, they used writings I produced to read out to courses in Westminster.'

Shane began working there in September 1974, when he was 16 years old. The institution was housed in an old Victorian building next to Cadby Hall, the famous Lyons factory, and the aroma of cakes and biscuits filled the air. It primarily served the local neighbourhood, creating a melting pot of young people from many ethnic backgrounds, particularly West Indian and London Irish. Shane had no interest in studying, and enrolling in A-levels was more about soothing his mother than gratifying any intellectual drive on his own. His world continued to revolve on using pot and taking LSD in his bedroom, while expanding his record collection and understanding of the music scene. And it was because of this obsession that he met classmate Bernie France, who would become a lifetime buddy. Bernie was about a year older than Shane and had been expelled from two different schools before ending up at Hammersmith. When they first met, they were in an art class, and Shane's unusual appearance stood out. "We were creating a still-life on a table when this guy steps in, incredibly thin, very tall, dead white face and long hair, dressed in a style I wouldn't call hippie but a freak. Freaks were drawn to bands who were not hippy but revolutionary, such as The Deviants, Pink Fairies, and, to a lesser extent, Hawkwind... He wore a sort of school jacket, a choker around his neck, incredibly tiny trousers, and sharp boots. OK, I thought. So we're drawing, and at the conclusion of class, he comes over and draws me. 'I was dressed in a Dr Feelgood sort of style, with an untidy mullet and a leather jacket with a suit lapel, a little Life On Mars, I suppose.'When we started talking, my first question was, "What music do you like?" I knew he was going to say something like, "The Stooges, the Pink Fairies," so we hit it off right away! Then we ran into another of my friends, Anthony Goodrich, whose nickname was Moysy Boys, a guy from Maida Vale I had known for years. In the first couple of weeks, Shane and I were hanging out and spotted a guy with NAME and the headline was MOTT THE HOOPLE SPLIT, so we were like, "Oh, come here, I want to read that." I was staring at him, and he had a peculiar appearance, so I asked, "Did you live in Maida Vale, and is your name Anthony?" and it was him. Shane's attendance was irregular, and he appeared less and less as the year progressed. When he was in college, the conversation was always about music, and they read the music press from cover to cover to learn more about the bands they were interested in. In 1974, David Bowie released Diamond Dogs, and glam acts like Roxy Music, The Sweet, and Slade stamped their platform boots all over the UK Top 40. Shane and Bernie were more interested in bands redefining the boundaries of rock on the other side of the Atlantic. They were both fans of the MC5 and The Stooges, two Michigan bands whose insurgency and white-hot fury would stoke the flames of punk. The Flamin' Groovies and Velvet Underground had also arrived on their radar, and the music press was the only source of information on these trailblazing artists. Shane and Bernie were always drawing. They were influenced by 'very violent and psychedelic' underground comics including works by American artists such as S. Clay Wilson and Robert Crumb. They designed their own posters and album sleeves in the absence of images of bands like MC5. They also briefly formed their own band, the name of which became the title of a song performed by The Nips and The Pogues.

"We created Hot Dogs With Everything, but we never damaged it by putting it into action!' Bernie explains. 'It was an idea, and we came up with song titles and album covers. It was just me, Shane, Charlie, and anyone else around at the moment. It was always "on the verge of happening." We didn't need instruments because we were bashing on tables and singing to one another. I'm sure I'd have played guitar.' Shane continued to visit Tipperary whenever he could, and his cousin Lisa Mulvihill recalls feeling threatened by him. 'Because he was ten years older than me, I was always a little terrified of Shane,' she recalls. So, when he returned at 16 and was a punk rocker, I was maybe 6 or 7 years old. I was scared. All I can remember is him sitting on the floor, with incredibly long nails and really artistic hands, strumming the guitar.' 'When he initially came during his teenage years, he had his hair quite long and he would wear Uncle John's vests and combat jackets,' Debra Donnelly recalls. Shane and his pals were regulars at the Camden Roundhouse's Implosion nights on Sundays. Freaks of all ages descended on light shows to witness an exotic lineup of acts such as Hawkwind and the Pink Fairies. These subterranean events began at three o'clock in the afternoon, attracting long lines that snaked around the venue on Chalk Farm Road. DJ Jeff Dexter's legendary, LSD-fueled events not only featured some of rock's biggest names, but they also served as a crucible for those who would lead the revolution that was to come. Mick Jones of The Clash, John Lydon of the Sex Pistols, and Poly Styrene of X-Ray Spex were among those lured to these continuous music sessions by Shane. Even on these hallucinogenic Sunday afternoons, when ice cream was served and people lay down under the strobe lights, Shane was still targeted because of his appearance and behaviour, according to Bernie. 'There were factions, it was violent, and if you didn't look the correct way...' Shane, in particular, used to get a lot of kicks because of how he looked and how he reacted to people. I finished a couple of times. I know several black guys kicked him in Camden because he was wearing a rockabilly southern [US] flag.'

Shane spent less and less time in college, preferring to do drugs with his friends in his bedroom and attracting police attention. Therese was still battling with life at the Barbican, her sadness limiting her to her chamber on a regular basis, and she and Maurice had little control over their odd and wayward son. To no one's astonishment, history was going to repeat itself. 'The last time I saw Shane in college was on the day he was kicked out,' Bernie recalls. 'He was sitting on the stairs, painting a bebop musician on the wall with a felt pen - beret, striped T-shirt, saxophone. The college's principal, who was reading the classic Guardian-reading, "We're going to help the kids' " kind, just flipped. "Shane. You come in here off the top of your head. Get out immediately and never return!" He pushed her over the edge, which is fantastic. And he just chuckled and walked away... He was far more daring than I was; I would never do something like that. So I suppose I was starting to be impressed by his audacity.' Shane's drug addiction was not only the cause of his second expulsion in two years. It was seriously affecting his mental health. He was drinking as well as taking acid and a variety of medicines, creating an uneasy cocktail. He had hallucinations and bizarre things appeared on his bedroom wall, scaring him so much that he couldn't sleep. While the Valium recommended by the family doctor helped him sleep and reduced his anxiety, the other illicit medications he used continued to affect his mood and behaviour. Concerned that their son was on the verge of a mental collapse,

Maurice and Therese asked Shane if he believed he needed professional assistance. He admitted that he did.

'We went to a doctor on Harley Street, and he advised Bethlem [Royal Hospital, Beckenham],' Maurice recounts. So we went down there, and Shane found himself in a sort of home in Beckenham. When you went down to meet him, there were a number of 'out of it' folks there, playing table tennis to keep themselves busy. We were very concerned about Shane at the time. But he was his own man back then, and getting through to him was difficult. I believe he blamed me for a lot of things.' 'The doctor had put me on Valium - a hundred milligrams a day - because I had a nervous breakdown after my mother had one,' Shane recalled of this horrific period in his life. That's a high dose, but it's not as high as what he was giving her. She was on actual zombie stuff, wasn't she? Every morning, I would go up and kick her to see whether she was still alive. I was admitted to the drug ward of a mental hospital... named Bethlehem, one of the largest in London.'

Shane was 17 years old when he was admitted to Bethlem, the world's oldest hospital of its sort. Shane and his friend Pete had gone to The Hope & Anchor in Islington the night before to watch Ace, who achieved chart success with 'How Long' the year before. Shane's last night out would be for a long time because his in-patient therapy at the hospital would last six months. Siobhan was 12 years old when her brother was sent to the hospital, and she believes it had a 'devastating effect' on her. Shane was 'very anxious and upset' when they went to see him on his 18th birthday, but when Maurice and Therese asked him if he wanted to come out, 'he decided to stay or, at the very least, not make the decision to leave'. He didn't leave Bethlem until two months later, and the recollection of that visit is still agonising for her. 'That was simply horrible,' she says. 'I walked in and couldn't speak. I recall just staring out the window, with no words to express how I felt. That's how I felt when I came out and heard "Bohemian Rhapsody" on the radio. That song perfectly expressed the rollercoaster of feelings I was experiencing. That absolutely messed with my head.' It must have been a terrifying event for Shane. He was placed in a mixed ward with people who had significant drug and alcohol addictions and had to provide a urine sample every day to prove he was clean. Painting was used in occupational therapy, and patients were encouraged to talk about their addictions and issues in group sessions. Doctors allowed Shane to keep his guitar, and he taught a young girl suffering from schizophrenia to play. He was also permitted to go on trips with a nurse and claims to have fallen in love with a young Irish woman who brought him to see Man at the Fairfield Halls in Croydon and the film Jaws. In 'Dark Streets Of London,' Shane wrote of "the place where they gave ECT/And the drugged-up psychos with death in their eyes." 'Pinned Down/I'm Alone In The Wilderness,' a song recorded long later, also appeared to refer to his experience on the Bethlem wards. When the Pogues recorded it on Hell's Ditch, accordionist James Fearnley was left with a lingering impression of the lyrics. 'Shane goes on this diatribe about these kids being imprisoned in an institution,' he claims. 'I'm not sure if that was his own experience. But there was something that struck a chord with him about young kids and youngsters having their lives go tragically wrong and witnessing the worst that life has to offer, and I guess he'd experienced it.'

Years later, Shane would open up to his partner Victoria Mary Clarke about his lengthy hospital stay and his experiences. She told me that he speaks 'very favourably of hospital' and that he 'enjoyed quite a lot of it'. 'It [ECT, or electroconvulsive therapy] didn't work for Shane. They continued threatening him, but they never did it. They were all having a good time. Except his doctor was actually rather cool, and he was lucky... Shane was on Valium, but he was weaned off of it in the hospital, so he was on nothing when he came out. It was beneficial to him. He doesn't look back with remorse or wrath.' Others with whom he has spoken about his time at Bethlem say the incident left its mark. 'He was always afraid of being sectioned,' explains Darryl Hunt, bassist for The Pogues. 'I recall him talking about that when I first met him back in the day. His most terrifying experience was being sectioned because it was your own family placing you in a serious situation - pretty frightening.' Maurice claims the doctor who was caring for Shane was critical of his lax parenting and acknowledges he had little control over his kid. Shane, on the other hand, responded well to his treatment and was in a lot better place when he ultimately left. 'Actually, he seemed to get along very well there; he made a lot of friends, got friendly with people, and even played table tennis!' says Maurice. 'And the nurses were taken with him. A doctor interviewed me and urged that I be more strict with him. But I held a liberal viewpoint and didn't think I should tell him what to do at the time. But I did talk to him and told him to ditch the drugs and just have a few beers like me. I attempted to persuade him. He was in good health when he got out; he had cleaned himself up.' By the spring of 1976, the entire family had reached a fork in the road. Therese had had enough of the Barbican's concrete maze and was yearning for some peace away from the incessant assault of construction work. She made the audacious choice to return to Tunbridge Wells on her own. Michele Harriman-Smith, Therese's niece, paid her regular visits at this time and feels the shift was beneficial to her mental health. 'She stated she needed to connect with the Earth,' she says. 'It was only a one-room apartment she rented, with a small yard outside, but it was adequate. She adored it. I used to tell her about my issues, and she would tell me how tough it is if your spirit is disconnected from the Earth.' With Maurice now paying rent in Tunbridge Wells and London, he and Shane and Siobhan moved out of the Barbican and into a cheaper flat owned by a family with a link to Paul Harriman. St Andrew's Chambers in Wells Street was off Oxford Street, and moving to the West End put Shane in a better position than ever to follow his musical enthusiasm while earning a little cash from temporary jobs. 'There was an Alfred Marks temp office at the top of Tottenham Court Road, and you got in there early in the morning and sat and waited and got called up and sent off to a job,' Shane says. It could last ten months, three months, or a few days. I worked at some extremely nasty but fascinating jobs. I worked at the Hudson Bay warehouse, which is where all the fur skins are received.'

When Shane wasn't at the employment agency waiting for his next assignment, he was carefully rummaging through boxes of LPs and singles in Soho. Rock On in Chinatown's open-air market was one of his favourite hangouts, and he immediately became acquainted with Roger Armstrong, Phil Gaston, and Stan Brennan, who assisted owner Ted Carroll run the stand. 'They used to say he'd come in and dribble on the albums,' Ted recalls. He couldn't speak well even then... He resembled the cover of one of The Nips' singles: short hair, ears protruding, terrible teeth, dribbling, mumbling, and grumbling. He used to wear suits a lot because he worked in the city. I'm not sure if he was an office boy or a junior.' 'One day Shane stepped into the stall and he was a little shaken-looking,' Phil Gaston said. He had matted long hair down to his shoulders, thickly caked with something, I'm not sure what, and he appeared bewildered. He stated that he had been hospitalised. I knew he was on to something, but he was lucid whenever he started talking, and he just started staying about the shop.' Shane's family had broken up, he was out of school, and there was no predicting where his life would lead. This was also the year that Britain went bankrupt, and chances for young people were scarce, whether you'd been kicked out of college or not. But everything was about to fall into place for Shane in a pub back room.

Nashville was in West Kensington and had previously been a country music venue before joining the pub rock network. Shane claims he went there on 3 April 1976 to see his first show since leaving the hospital. The 101ers headlined, a four-piece band led by Joe Strummer that was already on the radar of Chiswick Records, the label founded the previous year by Ted Carroll and Roger Armstrong. But it was the first group that night that blew Shane's mind and changed the trajectory of his life. '...I saw the 101ers at The Nashville, and the Pistols were the support band,' Shane explained. "I couldn't believe it." It was right there. The band I'd been looking forward to, playing Stooges and Dolls songs. I simply thought, 'This is what I'm all about,' and I began following them.' Shane wasn't the only one who had a lightbulb moment that night. Pennies were being dropped all throughout The Nashville, including on stage. 'The 101ers had been playing for two years or so when the Pistols exploded onto the scene, and when I saw them, I understood you couldn't compare the Pistols to any other group on the island, they were so far ahead,' Joe Strummer remarked later. And I knew we were done. Five seconds into their first song, I knew we were done, like yesterday's papers.' Shane has always felt like a square peg in England. He never got far with girls at discos because of his appearance, and he was frequently beaten up, ostensibly because of his vocal support for the IRA. Despite his greatest attempts, he never felt like he fit in. His time at The Commons, where he always felt at ease, was priceless to him. He was and still is inherently shy, which made him feel uneasy with others. However, in his adolescence, he discovered a new emotion that would change his behaviour and attitude on life. Hate. The IRA's bombing campaign, particularly the terrible attacks on pubs in Guildford, Woolwich, and Birmingham in 1974, put anyone with an Irish accent at risk of verbal or physical assault. Shane's sense of unfairness at such discrimination would have been exacerbated by the republican songs he learned on his excursions to The Commons and the stories about his ancestors assisting 'the cause'. Constant news coverage of The Troubles on television would have fueled his hatred. When I question him if the 'hatred' he described to his probation officer was true, he responds forcefully. 'Oh, sure. For the love of fuck, it was The Troubles. 'They [the British] were slaughtering children,' Shane claims. 'If two or three young people got together, they were imprisoned in the Maze [a high-security prison near Belfast that held Republican and Loyalist detainees] and ended up performing filthy protests.'

According to Catherine Leech, Shane's profound pride in his Irish ancestry and desire to resist any discrimination began from a young age. 'When Shane returned from Ireland, he'd have a real Irish accent,' she claims. "We lived on the Edgware Road at the time, and Shane used to come and see us. We had an off-licence, and someone came in and said something about Ireland, which irritated Shane. He was a small man, yet he stood up and exclaimed, "Don't say that." Of course, the man had no idea why Shane was acting so defensively, but I don't suppose he'd been back [from Tipperary] for long.' The rage he felt as a result of The Troubles was combined with worry about his mother's illness, the schism in his family, and the deterioration of his own mental health. So it was a life-changing moment when he was abruptly confronted with the ferocity and nihilism of a band led by a London Irish guy. 'And that was when I saw God,' Shane explained. 'I saw this little redhead kid up there pouring beer on his head and smirking at the audience who were shouting abuses at him. And then he'd start this loud, rowdy rock'n'roll' number with obscene lyrics; I thought this was the pop band I'd been waiting for my entire life.' Shane's new residence, right off Oxford Street, put him in the centre of punk's storm. The 100 Club, The Roxy, The Marquee, and The Vortex were all within walking distance of the flat, while others required a bus or tube ride. The stagnant waters of British pop were suddenly agitated, and a frenzied Shane jumped in. Punk provided him with an outlet for his rage as well as a sense of acceptance and belonging that he had never felt outside of The Commons. He still drew notice with his outlandish appearance, but punk was inclusive and a welcoming home for life's outcasts. Being different was a virtue, not a sin, whether you were performing on stage or pogoing in the sweat-soaked crowd below. Although they were rarely attended, some of Shane's shows would become legendary. Jordan, Siouxsie Sioux, Sid Vicious, Steve Severin, Soo Catwoman, and Helen of Troy were already among its colourful cognoscenti, and on October 23, 1976, Shane MacGowan joined them. The Institute of Contemporary Arts on The Mall advertised the show as "A Night of Pure Energy," and it more than delivered. Snatch Sounds and Subway Sect warmed up the crowd for headliners The Clash, and by the time they entered the stage, Shane was in the throng canoodling with 'Mad Jane' Jane Crockford (now Perry-Woodgate) at the feet of guitarist Mick Jones.

Blood was streaming from one of his earlobes the next thing anyone knew, and NME photographer Red Saunders, who was standing nearby, began photographing. Clash gig cannibalism above the NME review, with a picture of blonde-haired Jane placing a gloved hand to Shane's ear. Another image beneath it showed Shane covered in blood and gloating while Jane lurched at someone else in the crowd. 'A young pair, slightly out of it, had been nibbling and fondling each other amid the broken glass when she abruptly surged forward and chewed his ear lobe off,' recounted writer Miles. After smashing a Guinness bottle on the front of the stage, she was about to add to the gore by slashing her wrists when the security men finally reached her, pushing through the trance-like crowd who watched with cold, calculated aptitude.' 'Rat Scabies - who I'd always insulted because I always called him a loud-mouth bighead - had bought me a pint,' remembers Jane, who would later play bass with all-girl group the Mo-Dettes. But I was wearing rubber gloves, and the pint just slipped right through. So, I'm not sure if I still had the shattered glass or if I had a bottle and, again, it wasn't my fault, but I managed to break that as well, this time with these latex gloves. So I said, "Oh look." We were near the front of the stage and may have been nudged. It wasn't on purpose. I was quite inebriated, and shoom... and the blood! I was sort of holding it and trying to sip the blood, so everyone assumed I bit it, although I hadn't. It was in the NME the next thing I knew. But didn't that give him a jump start?' Ted Carroll was also present at the ICA that night and watched the bloodbath. 'There was claret everywhere,' he recalls. 'It was near the end of the show, during the last number, I believe. The lights turned on, and Shane was bleeding terribly, but he didn't appear to be dying. I didn't think about getting him to the hospital; they were all inebriated, and I figured it would probably take care of itself, which it did. But it was fantastic publicity, and it certainly helped since there were images of him, and he was extremely identifiable with his flying elephant ears.' 'Everyone knows Shane,' he continued. Shane, on the other hand, is a gregarious individual. Because he isn't aggressive or pompous, he gets along with everyone and is everyone's mate. He was one of those persons that stood out.'

According to Jane, while the story was exaggerated in the music press, Shane never claimed it was anything other than "just fun." She acknowledges that she found Shane personable and handsome, and that he drew people to him. In contrast to Sid Vicious, with whom she had a close relationship, he did not have a violent side, and his kindness shone in the songs he would go on to write. 'If you looked at Shane MacGowan and Sid Vicious, Shane was like Joe Strummer to John Lydon: the angel and the devil,' Jane adds. 'You have two lanky, tall characters. Sid was terribly defective, seriously messed up, thanks to his junkie mother and upbringing. He had a nice heart, but it was hidden. Shane, on the other hand, once he started writing, had faith in himself and was able to put himself out there. You just saw this great heart and this extremely beautiful beauty in him.'People would adore that, as well as being around him. He shone brightly. That night, we were having a sparkling moment before I drank too much and possibly fell down. I'm not sure what happened after that. I'm at a loss for words. But we were having a wonderful time, and he was a lot of fun.'I had some great times with Sid as well, but not as many. They were more violent toward others. I also showed him how to be violent. Shane was not a violent person. I did. I grew up attending football games and chasing down people. I'd run alongside the boys. Shane, I believe, took a completely different path because of the music, but Sid never reached that point. He couldn't express himself through words or music.' Shane's renown skyrocketed with the publication of the story, and within a few weeks, the self-styled 'Shane O'Hooligan' had launched his own punk journal, Bondage. He hand wrote all six pages on foolscap paper and used safety pins to connect photos torn from the music press. During the time, Jon Savage, who eventually penned England's Dreaming, was selling his own zine, London's Outrage, at punk shows and had met Shane during a Damned show at The Hope & Anchor. He had free access to a photocopy, so he copied it for Shane, who then went around to places he knew and got it printed in exchange for some free copies. A press photographer captured Shane proudly holding up his accomplishment in the Wells Street kitchen.

The cover featured a shot from a Sex Pistols flyer, as well as reports of teen band Eater at the Hope & Anchor and The Jam, whom Shane had seen at Upstairs at Ronnie Scott's and then three nights later at The Marquee. Shane lavished admiration on the soul-influenced trio, dismissing concerns that their matching suits were derivative. 'Pogo-dancing broke out and from then on things got better and better, with "In The City" for a second time, "Route 66" and "Faking Your Love"

[sic], culminating with Paul Weller going insane and throwing his amp to the people in the front who tore it to shreds,' Shane writes of the Ronnie Scott's event. I was tremendously inspired by their act's violence - it was fucking awesome.' Shane also used the occasion to lament the infamous episode of Thames TV's Today show, in which host Bill Grundy provoked the Sex Pistols into swearing. 'When did EMI or any of those old cunts put "public duty" ahead of their precious money or the security it provides?' he raged. 'What it basically comes down to is that they believe their security is jeopardised just because of what the Pistols represent.' Shane stated on the final page that it was handwritten since he didn't have a typewriter, but that "anyone who uses a typewriter is a GIRL." 'I don't enjoy fanzines in general because they're boring and unconstructive, but it's better than reading THE SUN,' he explained. Siobhan recalls watching the Today show with her brother Shane when the Sex Pistols dyed the air blue. 'When Johnny Rotten said, "Shit," she [Therese] just laughed,' she says. 'She thought he was amusing,' she said. Shane had become a frequent guest at their gigs after being blown away by the Sex Pistols at The Nashville, and original bassist Glen Matlock remembered him fondly. 'To be honest, Shane wasn't the most attractive guy in the world back then,' he admits. 'He reminded me of one of the characters from The Bash Street Kids... All the little gigs he was at; you'd see him at a variety of things. He was one of the only people present. He wasn't part of the Bromley contingent, but he could have been. He reminded me of Sid [Vicious] in the way he bounced around a little too much just to

attract more attention. I never saw him cause any problems.' Shane had been working for months after leaving the hospital and discovering punk, moving from one temporary job to the next. He worked at The Griffin Tavern, a major Irish pub near Charing Cross station, for a while, but he was much more at home on the opposite side of the bar. Between paid work and stealing from the back of restaurants in the West End with his friends, he usually had enough money for records and gigs. There were bound to be run-ins with the law. After bricking the window of Bourne & Hollingsworth, the huge department store on the junction of Oxford Street and Berners Street, he and his friend Peter Gates were chased and apprehended by police one night. The couple admitted to being inebriated and not knowing what they were doing in Marlborough Street Court. The magistrate was unmoved and imposed penalties and compensation totaling £340 on each of them. The inebriated antics were covered in the Marylebone Mercury on July 9, with the headline expensive night out. But, given his parents' concerns about his drug use and its impact on his mental health, seeing him embrace punk was a welcome relief. 'Punk was really anti-drug and anti-hippie, so we were happy about that,' Siobhan explains. 'At the time, he wasn't very interested in drugs. 'It was music, music, music, dancing all night, anarchy.'

Shane wasn't just a part of the punk movement; he was shaping it. Its unexpected boom had the major labels scrambling to catch up, and A&R teams were trawling London's clubs and dive bars for the next big artist before their competitors. Chris Parry from Polydor was keen to make it third time lucky after missing out on the Sex Pistols, who went to EMI, and The Clash, who went to CBS. Shane, who had his finger firmly on the punk pulse, provided him with the crucial information he required. Polydor made one of the signings of the late 1970s thanks to him. 'He came up to me one day and said, "Chris, don't worry about missing out on The Clash and the Sex Pistols, there's a really good band playing, they're opening up Saturday night at The Marquee," Chris Parry recounted. On 22 January 1977, Bearded Lady headlined the Wardour Street club, but the support act was the band Shane was always praising - The Jam. 'Everyone knows that Saturday night opening up is a dead zone, but I went and saw this band, and I was really impressed with Paul Weller.' Polydor signed them for £6,000 a month later. Shane was known in the band as the guy who danced about in a sweaty Union Jack shirt, and Paul Weller was keen to get it from him. Shane fought him and eventually sold it to him for £500. Not bad considering he received it from a tramp. 'It was a real Carnaby Street '67 job,' Shane explained. 'I wore it to all The Jam shows because I knew Paul Weller would eventually crack and pay me a crazy amount of money for it. He presented me with a Rickenbacker [guitar]. I was like, "No, I couldn't part with it." I'd gotten it from an old tramp. I was trying to squeeze the most I could out of him, and he eventually offered me £500. "You're done!" I exclaimed. '$500 for a fucking mod shirt!' Shane was cruising the West End, energised by the bands who released the hatred that had been building up inside him, while his mother was recovering from a mental breakdown. Living away from her own family seemed unfathomable at first, but the relative tranquillity of Tunbridge Wells was exactly what the doctor prescribed. She was relieved to have escaped the continual racket of construction work at the Barbican and to be able to sit in a garden, breathing in fresh air. Maurice and Siobhan stayed with her on weekends, and every Sunday, she accompanied them back to London and stayed at Wells Street, where she saw Shane. Therese was relieved he had joined punk after the damage his drug use had had on his mental state, but she was taken aback when she visited one weekend and saw his new appearance. 'Me and Dad went down to Tunbridge Wells one weekend and came back up with Mum, and Shane's hair was all cut short and white-bleached, and Shanne [Bradley] had done it for him,' Siobhan remembers. And I guess we screamed - at least I did. "Shane, you'll have to get famous now to justify that haircut," Mum said as we walked out, because she had to walk alongside him looking like that.Shane liked punk because it had a lot of positive energy and he could do something, he belonged to something. It was incredibly non-sexist because all of the girls and all of the boys trimmed their hair. So everything was really great, and Mum and Dad had no complaints.' Over Christmas 1976, Maurice and Siobhan relocated to Tunbridge Wells to live permanently with Therese once more. Meanwhile, Shane remained behind, preparing to fully unleash himself on London's ferocious punk scene.

CHAPTER 2

KING OF THE BOP

Fireworks were erupting and screeching over the night sky, but Shane and Shanne Bradley's stars collided to the tune of The Clash. They were both faces on punk's fast-paced and constantly developing scene, with Shane enjoying newfound recognition following the 'ear-biting' incident and Shanne witnessing its violent inception. But it was fate that brought them together on Bonfire Night 1976, when The Clash headlined 'A Night of Treason' at London's Royal College of Art. 'I simply saw him across the bar with gigantic ears and thought, What the hell?' remembers Shanne, who was there with pals from her St Martin's College of Art fashion course. 'He used to be called Plug, like the Bash Street Kids character - and that's not a good thing to say. He was present. Because there were so few of us, you took notice of people. But it was already building up at that point.' Shane has been described as one of the first punks, but Shanne claims he was a latecomer to the party. She had watched one of the Pistols' very first gigs at St Albans College of Art around the end of 1975 and had booked them to play future shows there. She had hurriedly arranged for The Damned to appear at the institution after witnessing their explosive debut at the 100 Club on Oxford Street. The Hertfordshire youngster with the severely cropped, dyed hair had also adopted the punk DIY mentality, learning the basics of bass guitar from Johnny Moped's Fred Berk and The Damned's flamboyant prankster Captain Sensible.

In fact, Shanne insists that Shane first saw the Sex Pistols thanks to her. 'He was never into Sex Pistols back then. He was a big fan of Dr. Feelgood. He didn't even notice Glen Matlock and the Pistols. I took him to see them for the first time in Leicester Square's Notre Dame Hall. The second time they played, not the first. Shane had never seen them before because Sid was on bass. He said, "Don't tell anyone." Certainly, Shane's Bondage reviews of The Jam and Water came after his initial encounter with the woman who would play a significant role in his life. However, the blood-letting incident that had made Shane's name famous in the music press had occurred two weeks earlier. What is undeniable is that, as punk gave a fittingly tumultuous ending to 1976 in a Britain gripped by unemployment and suffering, Shane and Shanne were at its epicentre, yearning to advance from the sweaty, glass-strewn dancefloors to the stages graced by their heroes. Shanne (as Shanne Skratch) had attempted to start a band with friends Rapist and Claudio Chaotic Bass, dubbed The Launderettes due to the fact that their basic recordings sounded like a washing machine. But by the spring of 1977, she was on the lookout for new recruits and asked Shane the question he had been waiting for. 'He used to go crazy at shows, so I said, "Do you want to audition for my band?" and he answered, "Oh, that's my dream," she recounts. I've always wanted to be a part of a band." "Well, it's my dream, too," I answered. Shane needed little encouragement when he arrived for his audition at Shanne's freezing bedsit on Stavordale Road in Highbury, unleashing a torrent of energy and attitude. 'He knocked on my door, I opened it, and he charged in and started rolling around on the carpet doing a really excellent Iggy impersonation,' Shanne recounts. He screamed and all, and I simply said, "Yeah, you're it, you're the frontman." Perfect." He had the energy, that's what it was all about, and we got along great.'

It's easy to see why Shane's family was overjoyed by punk's good influence on his life. He'd spent six months on a hospital ward a year before, emerging with little purpose and plenty of rage. What he saw and heard in London's intimate venues provided him with an outlet for those feelings as well as an inclusive environment in which he was welcomed for who he was, very likely for the first time in his life. 'I believe I was constantly made to feel like a wanker at school, and it was always difficult for me to pick up girls at discos because I was so ugly,' he explained. 'I mean, the punk thing transformed my life. It didn't matter if I was ugly or not... nothing mattered. It was excellent.' Shane's band, which he would lead with such zeal, already had a name: The Nipple Erectors. Shanne had a dream about a band wearing rubber costumes with nipples after attending a concert by Jobriath, regarded by some as the American Bowie, and believed it would be a 'ridiculous name' for a group. They practised in her apartment for approximately a year. Drummers and guitarists came and went, but Shane and Shanne formed the core of the band and embarked on a turbulent romance. Shane was on the cover of Sounds in April 1977 as one of the "images of the new wave." He's wearing a jumper and a pinstriped jacket and is lying flat on his back on the floor of Harlesden's The Coliseum, his arm outstretched. That summer, he and Shanne were invited to appear in The Punk Kebab

Documentary, a short, low-budget film directed by a buddy from the International Film School. As punks flocked to The Queen's Silver Jubilee celebrations, Shane and Shanne were spotted outside Buckingham Palace with a sheep on a rope and the Sex Pistols' 'God Save The Queen' blaring.

Shane, at 19, has dyed-red hair and is dressed in an overcoat and dark sunglasses, whereas Shanne has closely cropped hair, panda bear make-up, and an old jacket. Shane is seen hitting the sheep's backside as they walk away. Shanne's buddy Joe Kerr then joins them as they board a train with the sheep and travel to the countryside, where pitta bread falls from heaven with the recipe for the ideal kebab. The sheep are doomed, and the trio gorge themselves on their kebabs, only to have the recipe stolen while they sleep by a café owner. The fifteen-minute film was relegated to obscurity, but it captured Shane in his punk prime: a study in surliness and hiding behind heavy shades, which would eventually become part of his signature style. Shane eventually made the leap from audience to stage before the end of what was a turbulent year for music and Britain as a country. The Nipple Erectors made their thunderous premiere on September 17, 1977, at The Roxy in Covent Garden, with guitarist Roger Towndrow and drummer Arcane Vendetta rounding out a line-up that would continually ebb and shift. "I would say it was one of the best punk gigs I've seen," remarked Mark Jay, a teenager, in the fanzine Skum. 'There was no barrier between the band and the audience... Shane, shaking the mic back and forth, cigarette end falling out of his mouth... Shanne on bass stumbles around half-drunk... Storming through "Downtown", "19 Wasted Years", "Stupid Cow" (about Shanne), "Urban Success", "Abuse", and then... "Poxy Poser"... Shane sings, "You're a proxy poser - you, you, you," gesturing to the sweating pogo-ers at the front of the stage. Captain Sensible walked in halfway through the set with a bunch of red and white roses, and we all started pelting the band with them.'

The Cambridge at Cambridge Circus was one of Shane's favourite hangouts in Soho. The pub, located on the crossroads of Charing Cross Road and Shaftesbury Avenue in London, was a meeting place for art students, punks, and scene influencers like Malcolm McLaren in the late 1970s. It was within walking distance to Wells Street. Shane and Shanne were interviewed there in October 1977 for a Skum feature. Shane appears on the cover, standing next to a urinal, cigarette dangling from his mouth. In one of his earliest interviews, he provided fairly straightforward comments. When asked about The Nipple Erectors' influences, he mentioned 'Rolf Harris and Cliff Richard,' while Shanne mentioned The Jam, the Sex Pistols, the Ramones, and Wayne County (later Jayne County). There was no specific picture he was aiming to project on stage, and he admitted that it was "bad enough trying to hold a mic." The band had no political beliefs and simply desired to 'make as much money as possible for accomplishing fuck-all!' The duo had tremendous chemistry on stage, and their connection was blossoming off stage. They were so in love that they almost married in 1977. 'We went to Finsbury Town Hall together and booked it and met with the registrar,' Shanne recounts. 'We were serious about it, and we were going to do it. But his parents called my mother and suggested, "Perhaps they should think about it, wait a while."'

When asked how she felt when their plans were scrapped, Shanne responds, 'I didn't really think about it. I just assumed it would happen later. We were having so much fun walking around town or just being in and making music. We just get along so nicely.' 'Shanne used to come around to our place and they were getting married,' Siobhan recalls. They were older than 17, but they were still very young, and they requested if they could marry for whatever reason. Their plan was to marry in gorilla suits. But Mum and Dad said, "No, you're way too young," and it most likely had an impact at the time. Punk's DIY mentality had produced a slew of competing bands, but Shane's fame as 'that man who got his ear bitten off' meant there was an immediate buzz of interest surrounding The Nipple Erectors. And one thing was obvious: Shane was ambitious. He may have appeared casual, but he considered the group as a serious endeavour, and he desired 'To Be Someone,' to borrow a Paul Weller phrase. 'If I don't make any money, I'm going to want to know why,' he said to Sounds, and he meant it. 'As quiet and sensitive as he was, he was also very confident,' Siobhan says. 'He had a lot of confidence and was really driven, and when you're driven, you don't care about what's in front of you. 'You're heading there.' Phil Gaston and Stan Brennan had taken over the band's management and ensured that there was no scarcity of engagements. The Nipple Erectors became a regular on the London live scene, performing at venues such as Camden's The

Music Machine, Islington's The Hope & Anchor, and West Hampstead's The Moonlight Club. They also toured extensively, and in October 1978, they made punk history by crossing the Irish Sea to play in Belfast. 'The Nipple Erectors played The Harp Bar in Belfast in 1978, which was the first venue to allow both Protestants and Catholics to meet during The Troubles,' adds Shanne. "We had a trip and saw the Shankill Road and the Falls Road. The venue has bomb catchers on the windows to prevent somebody from slipping a bomb in during the show. Terri Hooley organised the show, and we stayed with him and autographed copies of our record in his Good Vibrations shop.' Phil and Stan's management company, appropriately named Piss Artistes, did much of its business from a public phone box at the end of Gerrard Street in Chinatown, and they leveraged their network of contacts to promote the group and obtain their work. By 1978, new bands could get a single pressed and sent to stores without the involvement of large labels. Phil and Stan launched their own label, Soho Records, and booked the group into Chalk Farm Studios to record 'King Of The Bop' and 'Nervous Wreck'. During the session, the band looked worse for wear, and Shanne passed out in the toilet. 'Then I remember being unable to get up,' she explained. 'I could hear this dreadful noise, and it was Shane doing his voice,' says the narrator.

The sleeve featured a shot of Shane wearing a teddy boy draping jacket and exuding rock'n'roll swagger, but the record went largely unrecognised. A reviewer who saw them at The Moonlight Club in West Hampstead not long after their release described them as 'the sort of band who should care but don't'. However, their decision to change their name to The Nips that summer suggested otherwise. 'It was supposed to be sexist, which I never understood because everyone has them, but we had to shorten it from The Nipple Erectors to The Nips,' Phil Gaston explained. Three months later, under their less controversial new title, 'All The Time In The World' became the follow-up single. But it didn't fare much better, and Shane's open inquiry on the back of the sleeve, 'Why hasn't John Peel given us a session yet?' went unanswered. Shane may have been preoccupied with obtaining success and absorbed in London life. His mind, however, never strayed far from Tipperary. He wrote regular updates to his family, wanting them to know what the band was up to and evidently happy of the tunes they were performing. 'What I do remember is how crucial it was for him as he was developing because he sent Dad a tape of The Nips,' Debra Donnelly explains. 'He was really keen that everybody should hear it and it was crucial they were connected with his music. Dad used to adore it; he was overjoyed. Shane would constantly want them to know what he was up to; I believe he sought their approval.' He was extremely eager for Shanne to meet his relatives in Ireland, and she became the first of his long-term girlfriends to accompany him on a pilgrimage to The Commons in summer 1978. She recalls the long travel from London to Tipperary as well as the harsh conditions at the home. 'It was an experience, travelling on the train and the boat, and hanging out at the pub with Shane,' she says. 'I don't know how we got to The Commons after the bus went several hours to Nenagh. Except for his aunty Monica, we were all stuck there. There was no restroom and no heat. Fortunately, it was July, but it rained much of the time. Hello and welcome to Ireland! 'You had to go out in the fields and find a dock leaf,' Shane told me. They were living together by this point. Shane had left Wells Street for a flat in Hammersmith, but he finally relocated his belongings into Shanne's bedsit, which was immortalised in the Nipple Erectors song 'Stavordale Road, N5'. 'I believe I simply got tired of it,' Shanne admits. 'I have a diary from 1977 that has two or three pages of "Where the fuck is Shane?" We didn't have phones or anything, so I believe he moved in since it was easier.'

The band continues to perform regularly and seek possibilities to advance to the next level. While punk's unrestrained spirit had inspired them, their sound was more in line with new wave, thanks in part to guitarist Gavin Douglas, who joined in the spring of 1979. He'd been auditioning for six months, but none of the bands had piqued his interest until he responded to an advertisement put by The Nips. 'It was in Covent Garden, in a dirty basement rehearsal space,' Gavin recalls. 'Something clicked. Shanne Bradley, a young woman with blonde hair, was playing some amazing melodic bass lines. A man with large ears was yelling into the microphone. Shane MacGowan, famed for having his ear bitten off during an early Clash concert!' He was left nervously waiting after the audition as the band went out with their manager. When they returned, he was told he had the job, and their next show was at the Rainbow Theatre in Finsbury Park, supporting The Jam. Gavin also contributed to one of The Nips' most well-known songs, 'Gabrielle,' which was released on Soho Records in October 1979. The breezy three-chord pattern reminded me of 'Best Friend's Girl' by American band The Cars, and there were plenty of possibilities to promote their radio-friendly song. In January, they opened for Dexys Midnight Runners at Camden's Music Machine and Athletico Spizz 80 at Kensington's The Nashville. The following month, they opened for mod band The Purple Hearts and Stiff Records' Wreckless at The Moonlight Club. Eric works at The Marquee. When Dexys announced the second leg of their 'Dance Stance' tour, which would begin in February, The Nips were confirmed as the opening act on several dates across the country. Phil and Stan had high hopes for the band and worked with Ted Carroll and Roger Armstrong to secure a deal with Chiswick Records. Johnny Moped, Radio Stars, Drug Addix (featured a young Kirsty MacColl as 'Mandy Doubt'), and The Radiators From Space were all signed to the label. But when the label reissued 'Gabrielle,' it bombed, leaving the band depressed. When the press caught up with Shane, he made no apologies about it. 'It's a good track, but Chiswick messed it up, and I'm fucking ashamed to be connected with a foolish pop record,' he railed three months later to Zigzag. He said that The Nips will no longer release 'that R&B garbage'. His compositions will eventually zero in on individuals who lived in the capital's sordid underbelly. 'I want to perform weird dance music in the future - extremely strange stuff, but not fucking arty...' Trash is what we're truly about... the Soho district of London, which is full of pimps, whores, and junkies.' That month, following a performance at The

Rock Garden in Covent Garden, The Nips announced their breakup. Shanne told NME that the implosion was driven by more than just a lack of progress. They were sick of one other,' and Shanne despised the music they were producing. 'Shane and I were just not communicating,' she told journalist Adrian Thrills. 'We were always beating each other up.' Frustration in and around the group was deepening and when the recriminations began, manager Howard Cohen was removed. Shane was as dismayed as everyone at the group's failure to make a wider effect on the UK's effervescent punk scene. However, he had always avoided confrontation and his natural impulse was to rally to defend someone who was under attack. So, he was disturbed when that resentment spilled over in the direction of their ejected manager. When The Nips played their purported swansong at The Music Machine in Camden, Shane's friend Deirdre O'Mahony says, 'We shocked Shane because Howard had been terminated as the manager and everybody was extremely unhappy that they were splitting up and that Howard had apparently made a mess of it. I remember getting extremely carried away with that rage and being really fairly aggressive towards Howard, and Shane was really unhappy that Howard was being attacked. He was so startled that everyone else was so angry.' While Shane was left licking his wounds, Britain's music landscape was changing dramatically. The Jam, The Lambrettas, and Secret Affair were spearheading a mod resurgence, and youngsters were discovering Motown, Stax, and other soul albums from the 1960s that they had missed the first time around. Shane's musical tastes had always been eclectic, and he was as passionate about soul and reggae as he was about punk. He was still spending whatever money he had on record stalls and shops in Soho and elsewhere, and he was working in one as he considered his next move. Rocks Off (not to be confused with Rock On) had set up shop on Hanway Street, between Oxford Street and Tottenham Court Road. Shane could be found behind the counter when he was sober enough to show up. 'He could converse intelligently about any type of music with our audience,' Stan Brennan recalled. 'But his drinking - and at that point, it was largely drinking - was impeding his ability to work. He'd show up around three o'clock in the afternoon, stinking of booze and looking rough, when he was supposed to arrive at ten. I went out of my way to keep him employed. It was almost like a charity.' Shane's relationship with the lady he had once sworn to marry had unravelled in the same way that things had unravelled for The Nips. Despite her resentment toward The Nips' old managers, she remained close to Shane and recommended they reignite the group a few months later. This time, they'd be managed by Howard Cohen and Shanne's new boyfriend, former Madness member John Hasler. Gavin Douglas was not involved, and on June 30, 1980, tryouts for a new guitarist were held. James Fearnley was one of several who responded to Melody Maker's post for a "name band." He recalls being 'a little bit disappointed' when he first set eyes on Shane as he hauled his Telecaster into Halligan's rehearsal facilities on Holloway Road. 'I'd come up from Teddington, and when I went in and saw who he was - Shane O'Hooligan at the time - I thought, Oh, shit,' James says. 'But he was so appealing to look at, and Shanne and Shane looked practically identical - the two of them were a presentation. Shane was the one you were looking at, but not long behind was Shanne Bradley, who was rather menacing in her own right. But he was simply interesting to look at for me. I was relieved to have Terry Smith, who was playing drums at the time, in the room with me as a kind of conduit for this weather system at the other end of the room that could ground itself through him to me, allowing me to figure out what was going on.'

After that, Shane and Howard Cohen encouraged him to join the band in a nearby pub. James agreed on the condition that they find him a place to reside. Shane stated that it should not be a problem. 'I can remember them doing these auditions and Shane coming back and saying, "There was this northern bloke, but he was actually a really good guitar player, a bit like Wilko [Johnson]," says Jem Finer, Shane's flatmate at the time. James was now an official member of The Nips. However, his true initiation was still to come: a night of drinking with the band's legendary thirsty vocalist. The pub crawl started on Holloway Road and quickly progressed to King's Cross. There didn't appear to be a single landlord in the region who didn't know Shane – and not all of them wanted his business. That didn't worry Shane, who couldn't seem to sit still for long. Shane headed off to the next bar as soon as they arrived and ordered their pints. 'I wonder whether his restlessness the first time I met him for a drink was because it was so difficult for him to settle in one spot because nobody wanted him where he turned up,' James adds. The first bar we went to, the guy said, "You're not coming in here." So he was this peripatetic figure, moving about London and walking extremely fast everywhere. Not only was it tough to keep up with him that night, but whenever I went out drinking with him, you had to almost skip to keep up with him. He was always on the go, and he moved quickly.' Shane was chatty on this first night out with his new band member, possibly to impress James, and he talked freely about his family in Ireland and his experience at The Commons. The notion that it wasn't simply Shane's body that couldn't stand still struck James as well. It was also his mind. 'Something I've always noticed is that it's as if someone is constantly ringing a triangle in his ear and he has to deal with it while talking to everyone else,' James explains. 'Which isn't to say he's always distracted, but I think it's simply some bell ringing and that's with him the whole time.' The Nips' new guitarist made his debut at The Rock Garden in Covent Garden. They were still an unknown entity to him as a group, and as he strapped on his Telecaster, James had no idea what to anticipate. When he walked up to join Shane on vocals for 'Hot Dogs With Everything,' he was surprised to hear the crowd shout it back. But it was Shane's wild, Iggy Pop-like performance that stayed with me the most.

'Everyone in the room looked to be on the edge of their seats,' he recalls. 'Shane was wearing this smoking jacket, and he simply went off the stage and chose to have a paroxysm in the middle of the floor. It was freaking incredible. It was sort of like, "If no one else is using the floor, then fuck you, I'm going to use it and I'm going to writhe around in it." It was incredible. It was shocking but hilarious to see someone do it.' James and Shane found up sharing a property on

Burton Street, a dead-end street in King's Cross. Shanne and Shane had shared a flat there, but by the time The Nips reassembled, she had moved out and married John Hasler. 'It took me a long time to piece together what the actual relationships were,' James recalls. Later, when I stumbled across the instrumental 'Shanne Bradley' by The Pogues, I realised how devoted Shane was to her. 'Shanne presented to me as so impassive, and I want to use terms like cruel to describe her, but these are my projections of her, and they're probably not accurate. I thought she was odd, and that made me want to impress her because I couldn't pull anything out of her. The two of them were terrifying as a unit, and I was on the outside of it.'

Jem Finer saw The Nips perform and was very impressed with this rendition of Shanne's band. He believes a deal with Stiff Records, to which The Pogues would later sign, was virtually finalised. However, Dave Robinson's maverick label chose Tenpole Tudor instead. Paul Weller wanted the band to sign to Polydor and paid for them to make a demo at the label's Bond Street studio. 'Happy Song,' 'Nobody To Love,' 'Ghost Town,' and 'Love To Make You Cry' were all produced by him. Polydor passed, but Paul recognized the band, particularly Shane, and offered them to open for The Jam at a couple of their performances. The first was on November 3 at Leeds' Queens Hall, and the second was on December 12 at Camden's The Music Machine, where Shane joined Paul on stage for a cover of Martha Reeves and The Vandellas' "Heatwave." 'I always saw Paul as a type of mentor to Shane. 'I'm not sure how true that is, but Shane seemed to have a lot of time for Paul, and Paul seemed to have some time for

Shane,' James Fearnley says. Shanne was heavily pregnant by the time these shows aired. She wore a yashmak to The Music Machine, and the rest of the band was forced to wear her mother's nightgowns. Jon Moss was behind the drum kit that night, and he was unimpressed. He was at the top of the charts with Culture Club less than two years later and in a relationship with Boy George. Siobhan MacGowan was among those who witnessed The Nips' final public performance. 'The audience was gobbling at Shane,' she describes. 'He was all covered with gobs, but he simply continued singing.' Shane and James Fearnley did perform with The Jam at their annual private Christmas party at The Fulham Greyhound, but their performance at The Music Machine was their last.

The Nips had hoped that Paul Weller could do for them what The Jam's bassist, Bruce Foxton, had done for The Vapours after spotting them playing in a London pub. He had taken up their management alongside Paul's father, John, and their single 'Turning Japanese' had been a tremendous smash, peaking at number three in March 1980. Paul did offer The Nips the opportunity to record for Respond, the label he founded in 1981 as an English Motown. However, the sessions were never held. It was all over. Shane's songs were appraised by Richard Thomas, a promoter and friend from King's Cross. However, he claims that the UK's live scene was limited and overcrowded, and that The Nips became stranded on the post-punk swell. 'They were quite wonderful, but you never expected Shane and The Pogues would emerge from them,' he adds. '"Gabrielle" was a fantastic single, but there were so many of such bands around at the time. They became engrossed in everything.'It was a pretty little scene in comparison to what it is now. That was the case until the late 1980s. I mean, The Smiths never played in front of more than 5,000 people in our nation, and Joy Division played in front of even less. With such big bands nowadays, everyone assumes you must have spent endless hours at the O2, but it was nothing like that. U2 was always on a major label, while REM was on an American indie label, and they may have been the first band to play Wembley, though The Pogues may have done it immediately before them - and that's Wembley indoors... So The Hope & Anchor was perhaps The Nips' largest venue.' Shanne had a daughter, Sigrid, in March 1981, but she wanted to keep The Nips running and had some new ideas about where they should go. 'I'd been to Crete before and loved it,' she says. 'I fell in love with Greece and its music, particularly the Cretan style and rhythm, and I wanted to infuse it into the music I was doing. So I informed Shane about it all, and he responded, "Well, I would like to incorporate more Irish music." My landlady had handed me a CD of Irish rebel songs and we had performed "Poor Paddy" with The Nips. I was also learning tenor banjo and attending traditional Irish sessions. So, we had this little band with Scottish fiddler David Rattray and John Hasler on stand-up drums, but I was dealing with a lot of personal issues, including being homeless, and I just said, "I can't do this right now."

The Nips' time had finally arrived, but the seeds of what was to come had begun to sprout.

CHAPTER 3

FAREWELL TO NEW YORK CITY BOYS

The Pogues continued to play shows across London, one of which would prove to be a date with fate. They performed at the Diorama Arts Centre near Regent's Park on June 22nd. Shane and Spider's drinking buddy, Philip Chevron, was in the audience, as was Elvis Costello, to whom he had been preaching the group's virtues. By the end of the show, the singer was in love - but with Cait. 'I brought Elvis to see them at the Diorama, and he spent all the show exclaiming, "The bass player... isn't she wonderful?" commented Philip. As an innocent, I had no idea he fancied her and was hoping for an introduction. Anyway, he took it upon himself to establish his own links with The Pogues.' Costello was preparing to embark on a tour with The Attractions in promotion of his new album, Goodbye Cruel World, and he invited The Pogues to join them. The first event took place on September 27 at Belfast's Ulster Hall, followed by dates at Leisureland in Galway and the National Stadium in Dublin. Preparations were made. The band's stuff was transported to Belfast in one of Costello's trucks, ferry tickets were purchased, and Darryl Hunt arranged for a van to transport them to Holyhead. Everything went according to plan until they got to Cromer Street to pick up Shane. People shouted up at his flat after pressing two live wires together to ring the doorbell and receiving no response. Shane had not been seen in half an hour. James hurled dirt against the window, which eventually opened and Shane belligerently yelled down that he was coming. But it took another thirty minutes for him to emerge, carrying a filthy bag full of bottles, and get into the van. Darryl stomped his foot to attempt to make up for lost time, but they missed their ship and had to take a later one. It was a scenario that would recur throughout the band's history. On this occasion, James believes Shane's tardiness was caused by the expectation and increased strain of a huge tour. 'Every circumstance for Shane is stressful, even this one,' he says. 'However, the next one will be even worse. So Shane decided, "I'm going to stay here and not show up." I don't want to come downstairs, get in the van, and drive to Holyhead to join Elvis Costello's opening tour of Ireland, even if it means making my pals wait for hours till we miss the ferry." I completely understand. I don't want to put myself in a scenario with the least amount of stress because the least amount of tension is hellish for me.'

The Pogues were still relatively obscure outside of London. Their single television appearance had been on LWT, and despite the fact that the record had been published prior to the tour, radio play had been restricted. Opening for such a well-known performer was a tremendous coup. This was a complete UK tour, with twenty-seven gigs in halls and universities that dwarfed the venues in which The Pogues were used to performing. The final performance took place at the Dominion Theatre on Tottenham Court Road. Shane had little time for Elvis, and ties between The Pogues and Elvis' security team were strained. 'We almost got kicked off the tour three times,' Shane recounted. Spider did UDA on one side of the PA bus while I did IRA on the other. We used to drink their fucking liquor when

Costello and company were on stage. The guy was madly in love with Cait, which is why we weren't kicked off the tour. We also gave him street cred.' Shane was having a good time. He and Spider were an inseparable duo who provided endless pleasure. They were machine-gunning jokes back and forth and showing off their razor-sharp wit when they weren't studying world wars. Shane was also pleased with the tour's schedule. 'That tour came back to London every week, which was fantastic,' Jem says. 'Shane appeared to be in good health. He could do everything he wanted, including drinking, staying up late, and performing music. We had to live close quarters in a small van in less than ideal conditions, but it was all new and exciting. There were ups and downs, as well as the occasional argument, but it was a formative experience. It put us on the path to become a professional band.' Siobhan watched the band on their tour in London and knew it was a watershed moment for her brother. 'The first time I realised he was going to make it was at Hammersmith Palais, where they were supporting Elvis Costello,' she recalls. 'They weren't famous yet, but they were developing a name, and as I climbed up the steps to the gig, I heard the fans crying out, "Shane, Shane!" "Oh my God, Stan," I said as I reached the summit. Did you ever believe that would happen?" And he replied, "Yes, I did." Shane has an unusual proclivity for getting his own way. Sometimes his silence or a harsh glare is all that is required. At times, it is the sheer force of his case or the desire he instils in some to perform his bidding. He wields authority over people off the stage because he is charismatic on it. As a result, when the legendary figure of Frank Murray became the band's manager, a war of wills erupted.

People simply can't say "No" to Shane, according to Kathy MacMillan. 'He puts up a solid argument and stares at you with those huge blue eyes, and you think, Oh, what the hell. That, I believe, was the crux of his and Frank's difficulty. He was also a very charming man, quite personable, and used to getting his way. It was a battle between two dominant males.' Frank was a tough Dubliner who had managed the Irish bands Skid Row and Thin Lizzy and believed in his charges' ability to work and play hard. During the Elvis Costello tour, he met Jem Finer in a pub, and the timing of their talk was fortunate. The Pogues had no manager, and the majority of the responsibility had landed on their banjo player. Shane, after all, could scarcely be relied on to get himself to rehearsals and gigs. And, while the tour had raised their reputation significantly, there was little money flowing in. If they were to go professional, they needed to be controlled similarly, and Jem proposed they give Frank a chance. A meeting was scheduled in a Camden tavern, and it was agreed that he would take charge.

Shane was sceptical from the beginning. 'First and foremost, I was the only person who did not vote for Frank to be the manager,' he explained. "We had varied degrees of relationship with him, but I knew him better than anyone else, and at the meeting where we decided to offer him to look after us, he warned us that we'd probably all detest him within a few months. But I never disliked him.'

The Pogues took a few weeks break before going on the Lock Up Your Drinks Cabinet Tour in early December 1984. But it was evident from the start that there would be no respite under Frank's leadership. 'After the Costello tour, I felt I couldn't handle looking after the organisational side of things,' Jem explains. It was also too much for me because I had a young family. So we hired a manager, which I found difficult because I disagreed with many of his ideas. I suddenly thought, Fuck, we've just given something extremely valuable to the wrong guy. He had an old-school operating method in which you put a band on the road and they do nothing else. So we began giving tours of the country, and France became quite interested in us. We first went to France, and then Germany became interested in us, so we went to Germany. Any manager would have done it; you get everything running smoothly and then start picking up the phone and saying you won't perform certain gigs. That's understandable. So, immediately following the Costello tour, we began our own headline tours, beginning with tiny venues and steadily expanding as the audiences grew larger.'

The Costello tour paid off right away. On December 12, John Peel played a second session, which included Shane's "Sally MacLennane," Phil Gaston's "Navigator," and renditions of "Whiskey You're The Devil" and "Danny Boy." The following month, they returned to the influential Channel 4 show The Tube, which was followed by a five-week tour. Frank had quickly signed them with gig booker Derek Kemp at The Agency; keeping the band on the road as much as possible was essential to his strategy for selling massive volumes of records. 'We started getting a lot of concerts all around London and the home counties, and finally we toured the north and the Midlands, we did Scotland on a regular basis, and we did Ireland,' adds Shane. The goal was to play Irish traditional/rock'n'roll to as many people as possible, and the costs quickly escalated... Young, London-basedIrish musicians weren't playing sets in bars, but after The Pogues debuted, I was thanked by a lot of these folks because they all suddenly had a lot of employment because we made Irish hip.' Frank had also successfully arranged for the band to return to Elephant Studios, this time with Elvis Costello at the helm. Elvis was engaged with Squeeze's East Side Story and was responsible for The Specials' very successful debut. He was picky about who he collaborated with, and his manager Jake Riviera dismissed rumours that he intended to produce The Pogues. Jake checked it out after receiving a call from Frank and called back to confirm it was correct. There was no doubt that Costello's growing romance with Cait played a role, but the band nevertheless scored a victory. 'Sally MacLennane' and an achingly gorgeous Shane composition called 'A Pair Of Brown Eyes' were recorded as a result, and the results were breathtaking. So much so that Elvis volunteered to produce the next record, and Shane agreed despite his past commitment to Stan Brennan. Shane approached Stan and informed him that he would no longer be a part of the gang. Shane didn't specify whether he felt guilty or sad about his leaving. 'He didn't say much,' Stan observed. 'He kept it extremely low-key. A part of me wanted him to reply, "I want you to stay..." I'm not sure what kind of relationship you have with Shane. I didn't want to be hurt again after my initial experience with Howard Cohen and The Nips.'

Kathy MacMillan believes that as Shane became more successful, his devotion to others began to fade. 'I tell you, there is a trail of people who were a huge help to Shane in his formative years and he just ditched them; he went on and never spoke to them again,' she adds ruefully. And he's really cruel and contemptuous of what others have done for him... Stan and Phil, who produced the first record, were fired.' Elvis Costello was spending as much time as he could with The Pogues, which helped raise their profile. They accompanied him on a tour of Ireland during a break from recording, and he even supported them when they played their first huge St. Patrick's Day show at The Clarendon Ballroom in Hammersmith. Shane was sickened by the sight of Elvis and Cait kissing, especially when he was 'dry-humping her on the settee in the control room'. Despite the fact that Elvis was not the most experienced producer in town, Shane was enthusiastic about his involvement at the moment. 'I'm pretty excited about it, you know?' he added. 'I'm not sure how much influence he'll have on how it ends out, because we already know it'll be very different from the first... I don't think that implies it will be any cleaner or more professional, because one of the numbers on it will be the quickest thing we've ever done, and a couple of the others are also quite rough. You can still tell it's The Pogues.'

Elvis subsequently said, 'I saw my duty was to capture them in their decaying splendour before some more competent producer screwed them up.' The compositions that continued to emerge from among the stacks of empty bottles, cigarette packets, and other garbage in Shane's working space were as potent lyrically and musically as the Irish whiskey that was steeping his insides. They were vibrant and moving, with real, imperfect individuals. They also had a timeless quality, and many of them are still popular with fans decades later. Shane had discovered his early gift for writing in English courses at Holmewood House School, and it was evident even from those early writings that he had a distinct style. He'd written about war and violence, as well as life's underdogs, back then. He didn't sugarcoat his stories, and he didn't spare the reader from life's hard realities. In 'Euthanasia,' he described a son who kills his domineering father with a morphine overdose. 'He rose, laughing, then saw his father's deathly pallor, hurried over to the sink, and vomited into it,' he wrote. 'He then cleaned himself up and headed back out.' 'Lost In The Crowd' was told by a child who was pushed to the ground during the 1913 Dublin Lockout. 'He tried to rise up, but a cop's boot smacked him in the groyne, causing a searing agony in his genitals. He saw the blue suit and baton approaching him, and suddenly seas of darkness overwhelmed him.'

In his moving ballad 'A Pair Of Brown Eyes,' a drunken man in a tavern meets a combat veteran who tells him about the horrors he has witnessed. But, despite the horrors of war, he maintained his lover's brown eyes in his mind, prompting the alcoholic to recollect his own lost love as he staggered home. Shane's songs were now infiltrating the rousing stories from Irish mythology that he had taken up on his travels to The Commons, just as they did his school essays. The daring fabled fighter who slayed Cuchulainn's guard dog is reinvented at a modern dentist in 'Cuchulain's [sic] Defeat,' written at Holmewood, with rheumatism and in need of teeth. He ultimately dies in 'The Sick Bed Of Cuchulainn,' the thunderous opening track of The Pogues' second album, only to resurrect and demand a drink. Shane had always known he had a talent for writing. But it was an awakening for him when he found the strength that music gave his words. 'Westminster couldn't figure out how I could create a short story,' he says. 'What's the big deal about making up a story? things just writing things down, and I'm a decent writer. I can write, spell, and make it flow, and it was great when combined with music.' Two more outstanding tracks on the album were inspired by his time in London. 'Sally MacLennane' was filled with colourful characters from his uncle's tavern in Dagenham. In the meantime, 'The Old Main Drag' was a dreadfully dark story recounted by a teenage lad who finds himself sleeping rough and doing tricks for men in Soho's backstreets. Shane sang, "In the dark of an alley, you'll work for a fiver/For a swift one off the wrist down on the old main drag." The heartbreaking account, in which the narrator describes being "pissed on and shat on and raped and abused," made for an unsettling but riveting listen.

The lyrics were so vivid that it was speculated that they were inspired by personal experience. After all, Shane had spent his adolescence hanging around on the 'Dilly' [Piccadilly] among homeless people. 'Back then, Shane's status was pretty much hand to mouth,' explains Kathy MacMillan. 'Just getting by in life was difficult and unpleasant for him.' James Fearnley, who played accordion on the song, questioned if Shane had written about something that had occurred to him, but also understood that he could 'understand the experience of someone who may find himself in that kind of existence'. 'I remember reading in the media at the time about a boy who had come down from the north and ended up in the underbelly of London, and they found his body beneath a bridge,' James recalls. 'He was only 16, I believe, and the reason I say the north is because Shane always told me about the dancing bag in "The Old Main Drag" - that it was something they used to take to the Wigan Casino to change out of their job clothes and into their dance attire. Shane was convinced that 'The Old Main Drag' was based on other people's experiences: 'It's not necessarily about me... it's about what I observed. Everything else is just stuff that you see or experience if you spend a lot of time in central London living the - I don't know what you call it - "real life"... I don't like writing about my personal issues, as many populists do; I just want to give the idea of real life.'

Years later, things were viewed in a very different perspective. Shane 'became a rent boy,' according to Victoria's book A Drink with Shane MacGowan, which was released in 2001. Surprisingly, there was no mention of this in the book, and when Shane was asked about it in an interview with The Scotsman in August 2004, he was quick to dispute it. 'That's a bunch of nonsense,' he said. 'That didn't happen. It all started with "The Old Main Drag," a song I penned about rent boys. I know a few people who did it, but I never did it myself.' When Guardian journalist Lynn Barber interviewed him around the time of the book's release, he was evasive regarding the shocking news that he had been a male prostitute. 'I can't believe you were a valet. 'Who would pay to rent you?' Barber jokes. 'You'd be surprised,' Shane said. 'There are women who would jump over their grandmothers to meet a superstar, such as Victoria!' It was a lighthearted response intended to move the subject along. However, it was not a denial. A major clue as to Shane's personal involvement in prostitution had been left in a poem he had written a few years previously entitled 'No Half-Arsed Buggery'. He never intended for anyone else to read it, but he left a recital of it on a cassette tape, which he later used to record songs he was working on as Pogue Mahone came to life. The elegiac tone in his voice is profoundly candid, making for a challenging listen. Shane ultimately admitted to turning tricks for guys on London's streets during a talk with Johnny Depp and Victoria in the film documentary Crock of Gold: A Few Rounds with Shane MacGowan. 'Shane used to do it,' Victoria admits when the Hollywood actor brings up the issue of rent boys. After a little pause, Shane responds, "Just hand jobs." It was a job in progress [tsscchh].'

The iconic title of the group's second album, Rum Sodomy & The Lash, recalled Sir Winston Churchill's reputed assessment of the British Navy. Frank Murray and Stiff immediately embraced the nautical motif, dressing the band in Napoleonic clothes for a picture at Tower Bridge. Théodore Géricault's artwork Le Radeau de la Médusé (The Raft of the Medusa) was reworked for the sleeve to include the band members' faces. Stiff's marketing crew, ever inventive, went into overdrive. The HMS Belfast was rented for a launch party on the Thames, the band dressed in Napoleonic clothes, and music press journalists were plied with copious amounts of rum. Melody Maker's sub-editor literally went overboard. 'A journalist fell in the river and had to be pulled up by river police,' Shane recalled. He couldn't even drink his drink.'

The album was released in stores on August 5, 1985. It went to number thirteen on the UK chart in less than three weeks and remained nine weeks in the Top 40. In comparison, their debut album, Red Roses For Me, peaked at number 89 and spent only one week in the Top 100. The Pogues were suddenly competitors, and the 'Little Man' who had sung on the Commons table was now reaching his widest audience yet. Bernie France had witnessed The Pogues' transformation from a band on the radar of those 'in the know' to one enjoying mainstream chart success firsthand. 'They began to take off, and the last time I saw Shane, they had just published Rum Sodomy & The Lash and were preparing to go on tour in America,' he recalls. 'I saw them at The Mean Fiddler, and there was such a crush of people, I thought, He's moving on to another venue. I remember leaving and heading home, thinking to myself that I might never see him again. I didn't see him again for the rest of The Pogues' career.'

For many British record customers, a group who performed rootsy, good-time music without pretence was a breath of fresh air, an antidote to the fey, foppishness of the new romantics. The mood at their shows was one of complete abandon, a glimpse into the fire and intensity of punk for those who weren't there. And there was something rebellious - and characteristically Stiff - in making traditional Irish music chic. 'The Pogues created a space in London where first- and second-generation Irish could get together and just have a bloody good time,' says Shane's long-time friend Paul Ronan. 'Everyone was bouncing up and down. It was like being on a football field. People were just dancing or going wild in the back. It wasn't dull. Another thing I enjoyed about it was that when you went to a show, you'd meet a lot of fans and it seemed like a family. They had a devoted fan base, which they built quickly because when people liked it, they couldn't get enough of it.'

After seeing The Pogues on South of Watford, Paul decided to check them out at The Cricketers in Kennington, where promoter Jim Driver was supporting their cause. He was 'completely blown apart' by what he saw and heard, and proceeded to see them again the next night at The Sir George Robey in Finsbury Park. This time, he struck up a conversation with Shane, and the two hit it off right away. "We were both second-generation Irish, we both used to spend a lot of our time over there, and holidays were taken in Ireland," Paul recalls. We shared a passion for the same music, were influenced by the same bands - The Dubliners, The Clancy Brothers, and the show bands - and were just a year apart in age. As a result, we had a lot in common. I began frequenting The Devonshire Arms in Camden Town, and we became pretty close. I lived in Chichester for a while, but I used to come up on weekends, and when I had time off, I used to visit a number of the institutions. I recall the UEA in Norwich and Reading. When I spotted the crowds outside of the band's usual London market, I thought to myself, "Something incredible is happening tonight," and the hairs on the back of my neck stood up. It was an incredible sight to behold.' The timing of the band's entrance on the UK music scene made them especially relevant to the country's Irish populations, particularly those in London. Suspicion and mistrust of anyone with an Irish accent persisted, making many people feel intimidated. Nonetheless, Shane was as 'out there' with his Irishness as he had been throughout his Cambridge years. He was unabashedly proud of his ancestry, from the traditional instruments and songs he had heard as a boy in The Commons to his family's ties to the republican movement. Shane was thus a voice for individuals who felt ghettoised and self-conscious in Thatcher's Britain. He was a beacon in an uncomfortable period.

On October 12, 1984, the Pogues were on tour with Elvis Costello when the IRA attempted to assassinate Margaret Thatcher and her government. A hundred-pound bomb exploded in Brighton's Grand Hotel, where the Conservative Party conference was being held. Five individuals were killed, including a sitting MP, and 31 were injured. The explosion almost missed the Thatchers' sitting room, where she was still working, but impacted the bathroom and bedroom where her husband Denis was sleeping. As individuals were being dragged from the rubble, the IRA issued a terrifying statement: 'Today we were unfortunate but, remember, we only have to be lucky once; you will have to be lucky always.' The Pogues had performed at the Brighton Top Rank nine days previously, which caught the attention of the authorities, as did their reputation for singing republican music. 'After the Brighton bombing and everything that - we were on the road, thankfully - they came around to Stiff to arrest us because we played in Brighton a week before the bomb went off!' Shane recounted. They blacklisted a huge bunch of bands, and we were one of them.' Ann Scanlon, a freelance writer, was one of the second-generation Irish who felt empowered by The Pogues. Her parents had immigrated from the west of Ireland to England and owned a pub in Lincolnshire. She, too, had grown up listening to Irish music. 'My parents were the only Irish pub owners in the area, and the pub drew seasonal workers and those working on the Humber Bridge. It wasn't called the Nelthorpe Arms; it was Scanlon's pub in Brigg, and it featured a true Johnny McCauley, Irish, and country jukebox. When I first heard The Pogues, it was like the Sex Pistols had taken over our jukebox, getting drunk with The Dubliners, speeding with The Tulla Céil Band, and collapsing with Johnny McEvoy, whom I and Shane both adored. 'Shane stated that Johnny McEvoy's "Those Brown Eyes" impacted "A Pair Of Brown Eyes." My father had many cousins who were all Irish publicans. Tommy, his cousin, owned the Camden Stores, which is where Shane wrote about the jukebox with Johnny and Philomena singing. So that was a large link... It called to me because of my heritage, as well as because we had endured a great deal of racism. We did, it's true. I recall a harmless lunchtime conversation about what butter you had, and I proudly stated, "My mum only ever buys Kerrygold." And she went on to explain, "My mother says that Jacksons supermarket shouldn't stock it because all the money goes to the IRA." It's amusing now: my IRA butter - but I had to quiet up at the time. Following the Birmingham pub bombings, an anonymous caller called the police station and claimed that a bomb had been installed in our pub, and I recall being taken out of bed by a police officer. That did occur.' Ann was inspired to write about The Pogues after seeing them on The Tube and receiving vinyl copies of their albums from The Wedding Present's David Gedge, whom she had interviewed. She pitched the idea of a feature to ZigZag, only to be told that writer Kris Needs had already been hired for a phone interview. When he politely declined, she called Stiff's publicity officer, Phil Hall. She volunteered to pay for her and a photographer's train tickets, and he stated the label would cover their lodging and, more importantly, the bar tab. On October 31, she met the band in Zurich's Rote Fabrik and completed her interview in the early hours, as Shane emptied her minibar. 'My first impressions of Shane were that he was amusing and smart,' Ann recalls. 'He was an Irish Catholic from the countryside, and my parents are from Mayo, so we had a lot in common. He was obviously highly and beautifully literate, and aside from writing incredible music, he knew so much about music that it was an education. He was, however, quite bashful, which I believe to be a very attractive quality in people. He was a scholar and a gentleman in the traditional sense...'Frank Murray was late because his wife Ferga had just given birth, but he arrived later. So it was about 3 a.m. when Shane, Spider, Jem, and Terry Woods were interviewed. I believe I met Shane at an ideal time since he had nothing to prove. The Pogues were a gang and a family, and they were on a roll. They were like the town's final gang.' Ann had the opportunity to interview Shane alone for a story she was writing about the tenth anniversary of punk, as well as with other Pogues for Zigzag. She recalls him being open about his past. 'He was incredibly happy in his boyhood, the way he talked about Ireland,' she says, adding that punk was the best thing for him at the time. 'I recall him telling me, "Straight out of the loony bin, and the first thing you see is a band who look like they've come out of there too."

Shane is now a celebrity in Ireland. But this was not always the case. In fact, his beloved Ireland's initial reaction was nasty. Irish Times columnist Joe Breen criticised The Pogues, drawing a connection between his reaction to the band and that of current African Americans who preferred modern black music to the slave-obsessed blues heritage. Musical purists were outraged by The Pogues' take on traditional music. The Pogues appeared on RTE Radio 2's B. P. Fallon Orchestra on September 5, 1985. The show was taped in front of roughly forty people, including concertina player Noel Hill, writer and performer Joe Ambrose, and Foster & Allen promoter and manager Donnie Cassidy. Frank Murray was also present at the session. Fallon was an enthusiastic supporter of the group, but he was also looking forward to a spirited argument. 'This evening, we have possibly the most controversial group in the groovy world of pop and roll as our special guests,' he told listeners. With The Pogues and their manager in one corner and the purists in the other, the host pondered whether they felt 'a bit more exposed' coming to Ireland and if it was a case of delivering 'coals to Newcastle'. 'I mean, who expects the Spanish Inquisition?' When the inquiry was directed at him, Shane lashed back. Fallon then asked if that was the same as people naively saying The Rolling Stones shouldn't play Chuck Berry songs in America. When Shane returned as quickly as lightning, the room burst out laughing, 'Yeah, well, they were correct about that!' The subsequent heated debates focused on the group's Irishness and what constituted Irish music. It highlighted Shane's sharp wit as well as his great knowledge and love of Irish music. When Fallon questioned if they listened to Irish music at all, naming Moving Hearts and Clannad as examples, Shane responded, 'Well, I'm not sure if Moving Hearts are Irish music in general, apart from the latest album, anyway.' 'Well, what do you think of them?' Fallon inquired.

'It depends if you mean Irish music played by individuals who have lived all their lives in Ireland, or Irish music as some kind of sense of what the Irish musical tradition is or anything,' Shane explained. 'If it's the second, I wouldn't count Moving Hearts, do you understand? If that's the case, they're an Irish band. It makes no difference whether you're Irish or not in Finland or Germany. I really don't get what's so shocking about a group playing what we're playing; I'm not sure what's so perplexing.' Former Planxty member Noel Hill was irritated by the emergence of The Pogues, a band whose music bore little similarity to traditional Irish music and was sullying the genre's reputation. Meanwhile, he claimed that labelling the raucous ballad bands that developed from drunken sessions in Dublin pubs twenty years earlier as Irish music was a "terrible abortion."

However, fellow Irish artist Jack Costello defended the band. Ireland has elevated its traditional music to the level of sacredness that it was "inviolable and we can't touch it." Irish music was powerful enough to be 'used, abused, and attacked' on any instrument. Because of its history, Ireland had a 'huge inferiority mentality where, whether somebody touches our music, faiths, or games, they can never do it like we do it.' He applauded forward-thinking bands like The Chieftains for taking it from small, rural pubs to the worldwide stage. The tense discussion ended with Joe Ambrose criticising Cait O'Riordan's behaviour as that of a "pig" and accused her of refusing to answer serious questions. 'Rocky' answered with a loud honk into the microphone. 'Is that acting like a pig enough for you?' she retorted. Christy Moore, along with Andy Irvine, Dónal Lunny, and Liam Flyn, was a founding member of Planxty in the early 1970s, and he was all too familiar with the scepticism and suspicion shown to The Pogues in Ireland. 'When I heard bad reactions to The Pogues, I remembered how people reacted to Planxty when we first came,' Christy explains. 'At the time, there were two especially harsh Pogues detractors, both high-profile trad players, and I recommended to Shane that he invite them to join the band on tour. That would soon silence them, and they'd take the soup!' 'The musicians [traditional Irish musicians] all liked us, B. P. Fallon liked us, but that moron Joe Duffy despised us,' Shane recounted many years later. Noel Hill accused us of distorting Irish music and infusing it with profanity. Whereas I mentioned a few songs that are full of profanity but are funny. Technically, Noel Hill was a fantastic concertina player, but he lacked spirit.' There was no less scepticism when they appeared on RTE1's flagship show The Late Late Show, which aired on the same day as the radio show. Gay Byrne, the traditionally conservative presenter and national treasure, was also curious about The Pogues. Gaybo wasted no time in launching his own inquisition after the trio performed 'The Sick Bed Of Cuchulainn' for the well-dressed crowd. 'Are you the ceili band, Shane MacGowan, or the ballad group, or the punk-rock outfit, or what?' 'We're all of them, actually,' said Shane, puzzled.

Gaybo was undeterred, and with Bob Geldof watching, he put Shane on the spot. What did he have to say about accusations that The Pogues were 'bringing Irish music into shame' and 'playing up the drunken paddy image'? 'Well, we started out performing in bars and Irish pubs quite a lot in London, actually, and we did typically get fairly intoxicated,' Shane explained. 'Did you?' said the visibly surprised presenter.

'Well, yeah, sometimes. We weren't playing in front of a large crowd or anything. So he [a journalist] simply combined these two concepts, drinking and Irishness or London Irishness, and dubbed us drunken paddies. It's merely an image, a label to put on people.'

Shane appeared to be bewildered. He didn't, however, react defensively or storm away, as some musicians might. He just stood there disarmingly, hands in his jacket pockets, denying Gaybo his Bill Grundy moment. This was an uncomfortable voyage for a man so proud of his Irish ancestry, making his first appearance on Irish television in front of his family. 'It's a really conservative point of view,' Jem Finer said of Gay Byrne's statements. People in Ireland who impacted us, such as The Dubliners, believed what we were doing was fantastic. It was never an issue for me. Shane, I believe, was more sensitive to it and turned into what people were saying, both for and against it. So perhaps he was sensitive to certain people accusing us of bringing Irish music into shame. On the surface, he appeared to be overjoyed that The Dubliners were enthusiastic supporters of the band and his writing, and fuck the rest of them. Whether you like it or not, it is the position you must take. You can't really start whining if you project yourself as a rebellious and "fuck you" persona - and Shane was always someone who had his own opinion. And it didn't matter because we were on The Late Late Show, and the joke was on Gay Byrne, just like the guy in Covent Garden. He could have been the one who handed the Pogues' fledglings their big break. Instead, he was the guy with the fabric ears who couldn't see anything.'

According to Deirdre O'Mahony, The Pogues were met with distrust when they arrived in town wearing paddy suits and a reputation for heavy drinking because they were defying that conventional image of Ireland. That was part of the difficulties The Pogues had in Ireland when they first returned because people believed they were making fun of them and that it was disrespectful, which it was never.' says Deirdre. 'This stems from Irish sentiments of being made to feel "other," and nothing exemplified that more than Irish music. Not the nice Planxty, Bothy Band, Celtic music, but raw Ronnie Drew, Dubliners, uncool folk music that was considered as a bastard; not respectable enough to be part of a tradition. In Ireland, the distance was insufficient. When you're in the middle of your own culture, you can't take a step back.'

According to Deirdre, Ireland was 'trying to rebuild itself as a sophisticated modern nation' by the mid-1980s, and the entrance of a group steeped in the Ireland of Brendan Behan and The Dubliners was ill-timed. Others, however, believed The Pogues would eventually help Ireland's efforts to modernise and progress. 'I think it was incredibly essential for Ireland that it happened,' adds Deirdre. Phil Chevron used to argue with me about it a lot, but I remember Bill Graham from Hot Press coming over and, as I recall, we went to see The Pogues at The Hope & Anchor and he was really shell-shocked. He had no idea what to make of it. Phil used to swear he got it right away, but I doubt it. When you stepped in, it was everything that modern Ireland didn't want to be and everything that hipster Dublin didn't want to be.' There was no navel-gazing over how Irish The Pogues were or if they played traditional Irish music elsewhere. As Frank Murray's demanding tour schedule continued unabated, they blazed a trail across Europe, playing riotous gigs in the Netherlands, France, Germany, Switzerland, and Scandinavia.

Those in and around the band would recall these as golden years. Even at this early stage, touring did not sit well with Shane, who couldn't wait to return to London. He was critically unwell by the time they arrived in Malmö, Sweden, in early November, and he was diagnosed with pneumonia just before they were scheduled to perform at Kulturbolaget. He was admitted to the hospital, as he would be on other occasions, and Elvis Costello and other band members took up vocal responsibilities. 'When the hospital started treating me, they pushed paracetamol up my bum,' Shane explained. That seemed uncomfortable, yet some of the nurses were pleasant.'

The band took a rare hiatus as Shane healed before embarking on a Christmas tour of gigs in the UK and Ireland. Their larger-than-life manager was adamant that consistent performance was the key to commercial success. But his impact on The Pogues went beyond just keeping the tour bus running. Earlier in the year, he brought in Dubliner Philip Chevron. The guitarist had previously performed with The Radiators From Space, who were also managed by Frank, and he was brought in to fill in for Jem on the group's first European gigs because Jem's wife Marcia was expecting their first child. Philip didn't know how to play the banjo, but he made his debut in Stuttgart and later joined the band on a Scandinavian tour. He was hospitalised in the past after a marathon drinking binge with James Fearnley on a ship to Finland created a near-fatal reaction with his stomach ulcer.

Philip was a natural fit, and when Jem returned from paternity leave, he joined the group full-time, relieving Shane of his rhythm guitar duties. Shane was always proud of his playing technique, which consisted of furiously thrashing across the steel strings and contributed to the fire of many of the early tunes. While he was annoyed by the group's proposal that Philip take over, he confessed that it had become a distraction on stage. 'They removed me off the guitar, so it was just Phil, which was terrible because I was pretty amazing at Irish rhythm guitar. Phil, on the other hand, couldn't play Irish rhythm guitar. He used to break light strings every night, even though he wasn't hitting them. For a long time, having the guitar was beneficial to me, but as we got faster and faster and madder and madder, it began to interfere with my singing. I couldn't hear the drums correctly, and the timing began to drift, and it wasn't Andrew's fault. Christy Moore is constantly out of time, although he doesn't employ a drummer.But then I went to the banjo, and then to the bouzouki, which is ridiculously simple to play. It only has four strings and is tuned open. I can't pick through it and pick out tunes like Andy Irvine, as it's supposed to be, or as the Greeks do. But I can make a bloody good racket that sounds exactly like it should. I missed playing the guitar, but not the bouzouki, which I picked up after the guitar and flashed in their faces, saying, "Fuck you, assholes." "Now, Terry, tell me how to tune this sucker!" Terry Woods was the second of Frank Murray's buddies to join the band, and his cittern was important in the creation of The Pogues' sound. He was an accomplished musician in Ireland who had been at the forefront of electric folk. He was a Dubliner who appreciated American country music as well as folk and other types. Sweeney's

Men, a popular traditional Irish trio, released a version of the Pogues' favourite 'Waxies Dargle'. He was a founding member of Steeleye Span, together with his partner Gay, and had briefly played with the experimental Dr Strangely Strange. The Woods Band was created later, and they performed as a duet until they split up. When his old friend Frank suggested he join The Pogues, he ended a five-year vacation from the music business. Terry's initiation was a trial by fire. The band was hesitant to accept him as a member, and a first practice in London did not go well. The next day, he was embroiled in an acrimonious dispute on RTE radio, with B. P. Fallon demanded to know whether he was joining the band or not. He replied that they hadn't asked. But they did, and he found The Pogues intriguing precisely because they ventured so joyfully outside the usual tramlines of Irish music. 'Funnily enough, the music I began playing was American mountain music,' Terry explains. 'My upbringing with the Christian Brothers turned me off to Irish music altogether. They irritated me to no end. That's why I never got involved with Comhaltas [an organisation established to promote and preserve Irish music] or the whole trad stuff. I hear the music, but I also hear offshoots, and I'm not interested in "playing note for note what my granny played, and if she didn't play it that way, it's not good enough." I'd play it, but I want to be free.' The Pogues were the darlings of the music press by the end of 1985. Rum Sodomy & The Lash was chosen the second best album of the year by Melody Maker, and Shane was crowned Chap of the Year. The NME named 'A Pair Of Brown Eyes' the ninth greatest single and the eighth best album of the year, and The Pogues had four tracks in John Peel's famed Festive 50. Phil Hall of Stiff was named Press Officer of the Year by Music Week for his inventive marketing of the LP.

Christmas provided a much-needed reprieve from the nonstop gigging. But only for a short time. On Boxing Day, the group travelled to Ireland for a tour that began at The Bridge Hotel in Waterford. Darryl Hunt stepped in at the last minute after Cait got her dates mixed up and missed the flight. He played with his back to the audience, reading bass charts scrawled down and taped to an amp. She did make it in time for the next event in Tralee, and she was beaming as she displayed her beautiful diamond and emerald engagement ring. Shane's victorious return to Ireland with the current band was a source of great joy for his relatives. He constantly made sure they were up to date on what he was doing and provided them tickets to his gigs. As his aunty Vicky recounts, a very special gig was also planned in a village in Tipperary, close to his beloved Carney: 'Shane and The Pogues came to Kennedy's pub in Puckane and gave a show there and everybody was just astonished!' Shane had never visited the United States despite all of the films he had watched and memorised. In truth, he'd never flown before. So, in late February 1986, he came to New York with wide, gazing eyes and childlike eagerness for The Pogues' first US tour. 'Kennedy was a major idol in my family, because he was Irish American and the first Catholic president of the United States,' he said ahead of his trip. The late 1950s and early 1960s were a time of enormous hope for everyone in the Western world, and America embodied that. Then there was a bang! The Vietnam War, as well as the assassinations of John F. Kennedy, Robert F. Kennedy, Martin Luther King, and Malcolm X. In a decade, everything moved from a dream period of wealth and everyone looking to America to the shithole that it is now. But I'd like to go there. I'm interested in all the varied cultures: the Irish, the Italians, the Puerto Ricans, the Japanese; they're all Americans, yet they each have their own distinct customs. For a variety of reasons, I'm enamoured with it.' The Pogues arrived at John F. Kennedy International Airport and were chauffeured to the Iroquois Hotel on West 44th Street. They had no idea how Americans would react to them or if they had even heard any of their records. Their debut performance took place on February 28th at The World, a celebrated venue in Manhattan's East Village with a refined clientele that may be difficult to satisfy. But they didn't have to be concerned. The city where Shane's idol Brendan Behan danced in the street had been anticipating their debut show with bated breath. The affluent and famous were clamouring for tickets, while the New York Times and other media agencies were pleading for review passes on the phone. Peter Dougherty, the man credited with introducing rap to MTV, was in the audience and captured some video footage. He went backstage that night to meet the band, and he directed the video for 'Fairytale Of New York' the next year. The occasion proved too much for one band member. Cait was on her way to JFK to catch a flight home as they waited for her to join them in the hotel the next morning. 'Cait was freaking out,' Shane recounted. She was young, and we were all young. She was 18 when we first arrived in America, and she knocked Matt Dillon [who would later act as an NYPD cop in the "Fairytale" video] down a fire escape! She was a powerful Irish woman who could be aggressive. She was adamant about her female rights and despised manipulation. And Matt Dillon wasn't doing anything like that; he was simply being kind and saying, "I think you're a really groovy chick," you know what I mean? That was the end of it! She kicked him down the fire escape, tsscchh, and he got up, dusted himself off, and came back up limping, saying, "I'm sorry if I offended you," and all that, and she said, "Oh, fuck off." They did, however, get along better later on. Costello had a friend there who helped her book a flight back to England, so he was clearly aiming to get her out of the group.' Darryl took over bass duties for shows at Washington, DC's 9:30 Club, Maryland's 8x10 Club, and a press show at New York's legendary Limelight club on the Avenue of the Americas, where Breakfast Club actress Molly Ringwald and New York Dolls frontman David Johansen were among the luminaries in attendance. Fans jumped on and off the stage and rushed the dressing area after the event at Spit in Boston, creating wild scenes. Joseph Kennedy, who was running for Congress at the time, and his son, John F. Kennedy Jr., were said to be discussing a fundraising event in The Metro next door. They went to watch The Pogues after learning they were playing. The band headlined a four-band bill at Lupo's Heartbreak Hotel in Providence before returning to New York for a curtain call at the Danceteria in Chelsea. The band was surprised to hear their new EP Poguetry In Motion being played on college and other radio stations in the United States, and by the time they returned home to do additional gigs, it had earned them their first UK Top 40 success, getting to number twenty-nine. The album comprised four tracks, all recorded as part of Elvis Costello's sessions: 'London Girl,' 'The Body Of An American,' 'A Rainy Night In Soho,' and 'Planxty Noel Hill,' the latter an instrumental by Jem Finer, but the others written by Shane. 'The Body Of An American' was one of the songs the group selected to perform on Saturday Night Live in 1990, and it was later used in the HBO series The Wire at police wakes. 'London Girl' got a lot of publicity, but 'A Rainy Night In Soho' was the show-stopper, a poignant, sweeping ballad that would melt even the hardest of hearts. Everything was falling into place. The Pogues' first trip to America had been a success; the press couldn't get enough of them, and they had their first hit single. In addition, respected filmmaker Alex Cox was preparing a film starring the band. He'd made the official video for 'A Pair Of Brown Eyes' the year before and was now planning a rock'n'roll documentary for that summer in Nicaragua. As the Pogues juggernaut continued, a punishing program of gigs in France and Germany was planned, taxing audiences and band members alike. However, these were abruptly cancelled after Shane was involved in another near-fatal confrontation. Shane and Spider had just finished a wonderful evening with Cox at an Indian restaurant discussing his current film project when a taxi hit him as he crossed the street. 'Shane was slightly behind me when I heard this bang,' Spider recounted. 'I looked around and Shane wasn't there. There was a taxi fairly close to where he should have been, and then he was on his back, further down the road. 'My first thought was that he was dead, but almost quickly I realised that he wasn't.'

Frank Murray, sensing the urgent need for backup for the now-eight-piece band, asked Joey to do the entire tour. The intimidating Dubliner with an athletic frame and a razor-sharp sense of humour had joined the group. He recalls first being acquainted with the band the previous year, during a long weekend in Paris. 'It was winter, and among other things, we went over to see Tom Waits. I ride motorcycles, so I was dressed in all leather, and it was chilly. So I went into the room with them, wearing all of my leather gear, trousers, gloves, the whole. When these people banged on the door and told me I had to go, I was like, "What the fuck? "I'm the only one who isn't gay in here." They were convinced I was thrashing them!'

Joey had spoken to Philip Chevron over a meal at the time and offered to roadie for free if his expenses were reimbursed. As a result, he was asked to assist Darryl for two straight gigs at Hammersmith Palais, including St. Patrick's night. He was then requested to accompany the band on tours of France and Germany, and he had his luggage packed and ready when word of Shane's confrontation with a taxi arrived. Joey had now entered the band's inner circle in America.

Joey had been with the band when they saw Tom Waits at the Casino de Paris in November 1985, and Rain Dogs, his breakout album released earlier that year, was the constant music on the tour bus.

When they returned to the United States the next summer, their concert at Chicago's The Vic theatre coincided with a performance of Frank's Wild Years, a stage musical written by Waits and his wife Kathleen Brennan. The troubadour, who was busy abandoning his drunken hobo reputation under the influence of his companion, was giving back-to-back gigs at the Briar Street theatre. Shane and the group attended the first of these before mounting the stage, and later that night they were left pinching themselves in astonishment when they found themselves drinking alongside their idol.

It would not have been out of character for Shane to skip out on an evening with one of his heroes. Anyone who knows Shane well will tell you that he has no desire to be among the wealthy and famous, and he can feel awkward on such occasions. He is far happier sitting with people in Nenagh or Tipperary bars than with A-list celebs, and would rather discuss a film he has just seen than his own work. While Shane sought achievement, he was never interested in popularity for its own sake.

When the hotel ceased serving at two a.m., Shane decided he wanted to depart, and they piled into a taxi and drove to visit the footballing icon. 'It was a fantastic night, and we ended up in a casino,' Brendan says. 'Giggs did not participate in the game, and one of the tabloids ran an article with a picture of Shane with the title, DON'T BLAME SHANE MACGOWAN!

The mood at many of the US gigs bordered on hysterical, particularly in areas with a sizable Irish population. This time, they went even further, with stops in Columbus, Detroit, and Chicago, as well as their first trip to Canada for gigs in Toronto, Ottawa, Montreal, and Quebec. The tour concluded on July 14 with a sold-out performance at the Hollywood Palace in Los Angeles.

The Pogues became the toast of America less than four years after making their debut in the back room of The Pindar of Wakefield.

CHAPTER 4

LONESOME HIGHWAY

Whatever physical or mental trauma he had inflicted on himself, Shane MacGowan, beloved by his followers, was returning. Rumours of his demise had been debunked, he was energised by his new band, and The Snake had demonstrated that he could still write songs that sounded like they had been around for a hundred years. Shane seemed to be in a better mood. But he wasn't. He was drinking as hard as ever, and The Popes made The Pogues look like a Sunday school picnic when it came to hard drugs. Shane had lost touch with many of his old friends at this point, and when he wasn't touring, he could be found behind the bar at his new second home, Filthy MacNasty's Whiskey Cafe. Gerry O'Boyle launched the street-corner tavern in Islington in 1993 and held hip literary events. The quality of its Guinness, its two dozen whiskeys, and the celebrities such as Kate Moss and Pete Doherty who could be found at its Rock n Roll nights, where writers read from their books and chose their favourite songs, gradually spread. Shane had long been known for his excessive drinking. He was the rock's Brendan Behan, writing about alcohol and drinking it on stage. His alcoholic escapades were widely publicised, and tabloid hacks and music journalists were frequently more interested in what was in his glass than in his records. But most fans were unaware that Shane was a hopeless junkie. Shane, like many addicts, would take whatever he could get his hands on: heroin, coke, speed, amphetamines, and speedballs.

He'd sit in his flat like a zombie, snorting one big line after another, trance-watching movies and drifting in and out of sleep. Siobhan and his parents' desperate efforts to get him into recovery and off narcotics had failed. The Shane they knew and loved had not faded, but had vanished completely from view. Sinéad O'Connor was one among those who witnessed firsthand the consequences of his heroin addiction. She had collaborated with him on the song 'Haunted,' originally performed by Cait O'Riordan and included in Alex Cox's biography Sid & Nancy. When Shane and Sinéad's rendition was published in April 1995, it reached the UK Top 40, and a drug-addled Shane could hardly remain up during the recording of Top of the Pops. Although his iron constitution allowed him to endure the massive quantity of drugs he was eating, others would not be so lucky. On March 6, 1995, the Popes performed at the Élysée Montmartre in Paris, and the band and some of the crew then returned to the neighbouring Hôtel Regyn's. A member of staff called French promoter Alain Lahana in the middle of the night. Someone was discovered deceased in one of the bedrooms. He rushed to the hotel and was shown to his room. It was Dave Jordan, the producer. He had perished as a result of a drug overdose. Lahana phoned the police, and after inspecting the site, one officer stated that the body had been moved. Although there is no evidence that the band or crew were to blame for his death, none of the band or crew were present to explain this or provide any information on their friend's final hours because they had already packed up and left. Dave Jordan was a well-known and regarded producer who had previously worked with

The Rolling Stones, The Specials, and Fun Boy Three before joining The Pogues' team. He had also been a heroin user, but he had gone to treatment and become clean. Dave was asked to produce The Popes' first record sometime after Shane created The Popes, and Terry Woods attempted desperately to persuade him out of it. Dave's wife, actress and playwright Elizabeth Moynihan, was also concerned about his return to Shane's employ, and she confided in James Fearnley. 'I'd like to think that we [The Pogues] saved DJ because we got him back into work from his rehab in Whitehaven,' he says. "I'm not sure whether it's true or not." But that was always my perspective. DJ was someone to look up to when it came to his life and his own body. Before his death, I spoke with his wife on the phone, and she told me, "I'm worried about DJ going off to work with Shane again and getting into that circle, and that he's not going to come back to me," and he didn't.'

The time Dave spent touring with the band and working on The Snake began to strain their relationship, and Elizabeth implored him to return to London and figure himself out. She had awoken in the early hours of the night he collapsed and died of a heart attack, sensing something terrible had happened. His death at the age of 40 filled her with remorse. Four months later, another of Shane's friends collapsed and died. This time, the emergency services were summoned to Shane's home, rather than a hotel room. When the ambulance arrived, two males were definitely under the influence of drink and/or narcotics. They pointed to a young man's body lying against a chest of drawers. There was no indication of life, and an inquiry later determined that he died of acute alcohol intoxication and opiate overdose. Bryan Ging, a young guy from County Dublin, was formally identified after four days. It's tough to say how this experience affected Shane emotionally. When disaster calls, he tends to close the doors and leave others to deal with the unpleasant or uncomfortable situations. He's timid and sensitive, but he's also an addict, and his misery and remorse appear to be masked by the exact narcotics that have taken the lives of so many of those he's known. Then there's the ever-present television, which blares out during his fragmented waking hours, forbidding any thought. His instinctual reaction to the death of relatives in Tipperary as a toddler was to face the wall and not talk, indicating a lifelong incapacity to confront reality. Addiction had taken the life of another of Shane's buddies, Pogues lighting engineer Paul Verner, by the time of Dave Jordan's tragic overdose. In October 1991, he died of alcoholism, inspired the lyric 'you wouldn't expect anyone to go and fucking die' in James Fearnley's song 'Drunken Boat' from The Pogues' album Waiting For Herb. Charlie MacLennan died in his sleep from a heart attack in 1996. He had been up all night celebrating his birthday, and his bloodstream included traces of alcohol, heroin, cocaine, and cannabis. He was 44. Shane's life must have been shattered by Charlie's death. After he left The Pogues, they became inseparable, living under the same roof and using drugs together. He'd dragged Shane's hulking form onto aircraft when he was unconscious, and when Shane needed a dose on stage, he'd meander trance-like into the wings, where Big Charlie was waiting with his supplies.

In June 1996, actor Tomi May observed the two of them while boarding a flight to Prague at Heathrow Airport. He watched in awe as Charlie and another man pulled Shane onto the plane and tossed him into a neighbouring aisle seat. When the plane took off, Shane was slumped forward, drooling, and three little vodkas were placed on the tray in front of him. He and Charlie began babbling to each other in 'their own pissed-up lingo' when he awoke. They had been granted backstage access to the festival where The Popes were on the same bill as Iggy Pop by the time they arrived in Prague, where Tomi and his friend Jay Chappell were DJing. They witnessed Shane and Charlie double-act in action again while watching the show at Koupit Džbán. Shane had slid more and further away from his family and people who cared for him by the time The Popes came to record their second album, The Crock Of Gold. He'd also lost something he'd always valued: friends he could rely on. Something else had also occurred that had completely shook Shane's world. He and Victoria had split up ten years after they originally met. He was heartbroken without her. So much so that he talked about his agony, which was unusual for him. 'Shane and Victoria split up at the same time I split up with my missus,' Bob explains. 'She [Victoria] was dating some young guy, so Shane and I were on each other's shoulders for a few months. "I know what she's about, but I don't give a shit," he told me. I simply want her back. She is free to do whatever she wants."'

Shane and Victoria's love may appear miraculous for two people who appear so dissimilar. Shane seems unconcerned with celebrity, despite the fact that she openly admits to desiring it. He drinks all day and seldom eats. Victoria does yoga and works out at the gym. They are, nonetheless, linked by a fundamental mutual desire. If Shane's anguish was hidden behind the dark shades he wore, it was revealed in his writing. He wore his heart on his sleeve in 'Victoria,' making a thinly veiled but sarcastic reference to her affair with Van Morrison. 'Victoria, you abandoned me in opium euphoria/With a fat monk singing Gloria,' she says. Their romance had failed before and would fail again. But everytime they were apart, Shane yearned for her return. He simply couldn't live without her, and despite the pain caused by his infidelity, she couldn't abandon him. 'You get irritated when you're so close, but it doesn't separate you,' she explained. 'It's just the way of life with all the opportunities and being on the road. I'm a really jealous person, but we've always ended up together.'

In January 2009, Victoria revealed one of the reasons for her attraction to Shane in a profoundly personal story for the Guardian's family section. 'Looking for a Father Figure' described her difficult and perplexing upbringing in a remote corner of Ireland, as well as her hunt for the biological father she had never met. Victoria was only one year old when her mother, Orla, married Dardis Clarke when she was pregnant with her sister Vanessa. Later, her mother informed them both that he was their father. When Victoria was about 7, her mother left him, and a guy named Dave, with whom her mother was expecting a child, took over as father. Victoria stated that she made his life "as unpleasant as possible," and that "we warmed to one another only after I left home."

Shane drank slowly while his friends guzzled their pints, but he made up for it with his large orders, filling a full table with his own beverages. When Shane wasn't there, the cottage sat vacant. The neighbours would be taken aback when he returned after a long absence. "We were playing LPs and drinking away when this woman barged in the door and asked, "What are you doing in here?" Shane replied, "I live here." This is my fucking residence." She was my next-door neighbour, and she had noticed my car outside and assumed it was a break-in. It could have been a year since he was last there.' Maurice and Therese had returned to Tipperary in 1988 after spending more than thirty years in England. Siobhan and her mother had taken control of the house-hunting and had fallen in love with a large detached house on an acre of land in Garryard East, Silvermines, a few miles south of Nenagh. They presented it to Maurice as a done deal, and he agreed to purchase it. Shane had begun creating songs for The Crock Of Gold in his bedroom there, as an escape from the distractions of London. He felt more at home in Nenagh and its surroundings than anywhere else, and the lyrics reflect that. He wrote in 'Back In The County Hell', 'When I've done my patriotic duty/And burned London to the ground/I'll come back home to Nenagh/And get pissed every night in town.' In 'Mother Mo Chroi,' he reflects on the anguish suffered by those of his parents' generation who had to leave Ireland to pursue work, as well as his own 'furious attachment' to Ireland. Maurice ran his own pub, 'Mac's Bar,' in The Den, a downstairs room. After smoking was banned in pubs in 2007, the family joked that it was the only smoking bar left in Ireland. Siobhan spent a lot of time there as well, as she had already returned to Dublin before her parents left England. She fondly recalls parties and sessions held on the site. Shane would always be at the house for Christmas, no matter where he was in the globe or what was going on in his life. The drinks flowed freely, and music was played till the wee hours of the morning. However, there was no roast turkey on the menu. Siobhan would make a vegetarian moussaka for their Christmas Day supper because Maurice was a vegetarian (he is now vegan) and Shane was close to becoming one.Shane's buddies made the most of every opportunity he had while in town. Sessions at Philly's would last until the early hours of the morning, and one morning, a cleaner arrived to discover Shane asleep across a seat. She informed him it was time to wake up and offered him a drink. 'A triple gin,' groggily said. Philly's manager, Tom Kenneally, recalls playing music one night while counting the take in the main bar. Shane and a friend had fallen asleep in the lounge, and when Tom played a CD of the late Liam Clancy performing 'The Broad Majestic Shannon,' Shane awoke confused. Philly also owns a funeral home across the street from the pub, and one night he surprised Shane by asking him to assist in the preparation of a grave. So, in the middle of the night, the death-obsessed songwriter found himself unexpectedly engaged in a graveyard. 'I had a funeral at Terryglass, which isn't far from Carney and right on the lake,' Philly recalls. 'One thing I don't do very often is get out of bed in the morning, so I had Shane here at the pub and around two a.m. I asked, "Shane, will you give me a hand?"

'"What will we do?" he asks.

'"A bit of an undertaking," I admit.

"Oh, Jesus, no bother," he says.

'So we went down to Terryglass in the middle of the night. We had all these rolls of carpet, and we all adorned the tomb! He fucking adored that. Shane wishes he could be anything other than a musician.'

Bank Cards are foreign to Shane, and his approach to money harkens back to his childhood in rural Ireland. Noel once escorted him to a bank in Nenagh to withdraw funds. Shane murmured to the cashier that he needed to withdraw some cash, and she told him that he needed to contact his bank in London to verify his identity. What followed was vintage Shane. Shane then went to a shop and bought a holdall, which he used to enter a second-hand bookshop. He walked up and down the rows, randomly selecting books from the shelves and stuffing them into his bag. After paying, he called Philly at the tavern and had drinks delivered to The Commons. Shane then read through his stack of books for three weeks straight. Unsurprisingly, the record was not as highly regarded as its predecessor and did not fare as well commercially. The Crock Of Gold, released in November 1997, peaked at number 59 in the UK chart before sinking like a stone. 'Justly commended for the uniqueness of his lyrics with The Pogues by the likes of Christy Moore on a recent BBC documentary, MacGowan these days is mostly a master of cliché,' noted Neil Spencer in Mojo. 'While it helps that he invented at least some of the clichés - the tales of insane ceilidhs and ne'er-do-wells on drunken binges that his audience expects - his celebration of current Celtic mythology on, say, "Paddy Rolling Stone" is never enough to save The Crock Of Gold from predictability.'

ZTT released 'Lonesome Highway' as a single, but it failed to chart in the Top 75, and 'Rock'n'roll Paddy' followed suit. However, by the late 1990s, CD singles had lost their lustre for bands like The Popes, failing to have the same impact as their vinyl counterparts. The Popes had previously released the Christmas Party EP, which included the songs "Christmas Lullaby," "Paddy Rolling Stone," "Hippy Hippy Shake," and "Danny Boy." However, its highest chart position was eighty-six, demonstrating that even Shane's Christmas release might be a festive turkey.

Before the end of the year, he did, however, appear on a number one record for the first and only time in his career. 'Perfect Day' by Lou Reed was recorded to benefit BBC Children in Need. Shane was joined on the charity record by Bono, David Bowie, Elton John, Emmylou Harris, and Tammy Wynette, among others. It debuted at number one and stayed there for thirteen weeks. The Popes' popularity was fuelled more by their live performances and the fans' love of Shane than by record sales. Despite the fact that The Pogues' never-ending travels had taken its toll on Shane, The Popes continued to tour with him until 2005. From the Montreux Jazz Festival in Switzerland to Pinkpop in the Netherlands to the Byron Bay Bluesfest in Australia, they were a great draw at festivals all over the world. They never had the same billing as The Pogues, except when they headlined the 1997 Finsbury Park Fleadh in place of an ailing Bob Dylan. Van Morrison was also on the lineup, and it was the first time he and Shane had met since his three-year affair with Victoria. Shane was beginning to consider the influence his lifestyle was having on his physical health offstage. Despite the harm he has done to his body over the years, he is terrified of dying. He is adamant about wanting to live and values the time he spends with his pals. When faced with the thought of leaving them behind, he becomes upset, clutching their hands for an extended period of time and crying.

'Shane had done the Olympia Theatre with The Popes, and he came down home the next day and remained around for Christmas,' Noel Kenny recalls. "Noel, this is the last Christmas we're ever going to meet," Shane whispered, and we both burst into tears. He was high on drugs at the moment, and you could see him with one eye looking one way and the other. 'Jesus, he's fucked,' I thought.

A piece in Hot Press in December 1996 struck a more upbeat tone, with members of The Popes portraying the time following Charlie MacLennan's death as "a fresh start for Shane." But their hope was misplaced, as Shane fell deeper into addiction. He sat in his rented flat in Gospel Oak, near Hampstead Heath, smoking thick lines of heroin and cocaine, numbing whatever emotions he was feeling. Before the decade was over, another tragic occurrence would shine a light on Shane's dreadful life.

CHAPTER 5

WANDRIN' STAR

Shane had vanished. He was scheduled to perform for the first time with Sharon Shannon's Big Band on December 27, 2007, but there was no trace of him in the days leading up to the concert. He was eventually found when one of Sharon's gang went out looking for him, and anxieties that he wouldn't turn up were put to rest. Shane made his debut with Sharon's popular live band at the TF Royal Theatre in Castlebar, County Mayo, and it proved to be a memorable one for a number of reasons. Joe Dolan, the famed Irish showband vocalist, died the day before, at 68, following a long illness. Shane was a tremendous fan, and when he received the news, he chose to pay tribute by singing one of Dolan's songs. The only problem was that he didn't know the song, but he was determined to perform it. We also had vocalist Joyce Redmond on board, and I believe Shane felt Joyce would be able to carry the tune and he'd just sing along. But, because Joyce didn't know the song either, things didn't go so well on stage. Aside from that minor calamity and a few minor teething glitches with the manner we as a band accompanied Shane, the event went off without a hitch. Sharon had shared a residence with several musicians in her twenties, one of whom was a Pogues fan, and she had been acquainted with his songs, studying the music from the ground up. So she was 'thrilled and honoured' to learn years later that he would be doing some guest spots with her. Her manager, John Dunford, had previously worked with Joey Cashman and The

Pogues, which had helped convince Shane to perform with the band. The band performed at Vicar Street in Dublin, Leisureland in Galway, and other major Irish venues. Shane was reenergized after working with such outstanding musicians and singers and engaging fans, some of whom had never seen him before. The chance to play and socialise with a new set of artists boosted him both professionally and personally. Coming on stage near the conclusion of a show was also less demanding and allowed him more time to drink backstage. Brendan Fitzpatrick drove Shane to and from the shows in his red van, and he sat behind the wheel with his own drinks table and fridge. Joey was still managing Shane, and they were an unstoppable duo, engaged in heated disputes and occasionally coming to blows. "We were performing a program with Shane and Mundy as part of the entertainment for TV and Shane and Joey were having a massive dispute in the van," says Sharon Shannon's producer John Dunford of their dramatic entrance at The Rose of Tralee festival. We were all at the site when they arrived outside the hotel where the Roses were performing their public relations. When the door opens, Joey and Shane are on the ground, and Joey is belting him with a cup, which he subsequently breaks, and he exclaims, "Now you've broken my favorite fucking cup!"

'Shane is a gentleman, and I enjoy his company. He rivals the likes of Burroughs, Kesey, Donleavy, Behan, and Hunter S. Thompson not only in intellect and talent, but also in their reputations for causing mayhem and chaos, enjoying a sherry or two, and not caring about perceived genteel manners of polite society or what anyone thinks of them. Whatever you want to say about it, I see wonderful honesty in that approach, and it represents the true artist.' When the Christmas performances came around, Shane would be dressed to the nines, with beautifully fitted suits and freshly shampooed hair. He would get to know and remember everyone on the road's names and buy them all drinks at the bar. 'Seven days later, he'd still be in the same clothes as the first day, with cider, beer, and spirits splashed all over them, having rarely seen a bed the whole time!' laughs John. Those in and around the band were also introduced to another charming aspect of Shane's personality: his reverence for the older generation and traditional Irish values. 'One of the defining events for me was one of the Christmas shows in Ennis when Sharon's and Shane's mothers were in the dressing room,' John adds. There was a tremendous music and drinking event going on, but Shane and Sharon and the two mammies were there until two o'clock in the morning, drinking tea and eating sandwiches.' Mundy was deeply impressed by Shane's personal warmth and lack of vanity, having seen Shane in The Pogues when he was 14 - his first live gig. They became great friends as the shows progressed, and to his surprise, Shane decided to sing on his song "Love Is A Casino." They recorded it one evening in a Dublin studio, Shane labouring faster and faster when Mundy announced that last orders were approaching. Mundy witnessed Shane's generosity after Sharon's long-term spouse Leo Healy died abruptly following a heart attack in May 2008, at the age of 46. Sharon was on tour at the time and was heartbroken. Shane had not returned to Dublin, and I was afraid that Victoria was worrying about him. I contacted her to tell her that I was leaving for some gigs in Spain and that I could arrange for one of my mates to drive him back to Dublin. I guess she thought I was attempting to kick him out of the house, which wasn't the case at all. She informed me that convincing him to leave Galway would be difficult, but that if I really wanted him gone, I might try sobbing. Ha ha! Anyway, she looked relaxed about it, and I didn't mind having Shane remain while I was gone. A few friends were looking after him, taking him out to supper and making sure he was okay and pleased. He was still there when I returned a week later. Despite the fact that I had created a new bed for him upstairs, he did not sleep the entire time. I believe he was starting to have foot difficulties at the time, so the stairs were too difficult for him. He liked to sleep on the couch, and when he awoke in the morning, one of my dogs was curled up next to him. She was a stray that I had taken in, and she was smitten with Shane. Dogs are excellent character assessors.' Sharon, like most others who get to know Shane, found him to be compassionate, sympathetic, and generous. She also sensed inner turmoil. 'When he performed "A Rainy Night In Soho," he would frequently point to me for the "Some of them fell into heaven" lyrics and then to himself for the "Some of them fell into hell" lyrics. That made me feel sorry for him.' There was disquiet backstage. Shane had gone missing the night before, despite massive searches throughout New Orleans and calls to police stations and hospitals. The Pogues' daytime slot at Voodoo Fest had arrived, and they had no choice but to perform without him. They greeted the audience in City Park, and Spider, as he had done so many times before, took centre stage. Shane was missing in action on November 1, 2009. He had gone out drinking with a Canadian acquaintance the day before. Normally, the band and crew would not have been concerned because Shane frequently left hotels and went out boozing with people from outside their touring party. He didn't have to attend soundchecks or meet any other pre-gig conditions, but he had to be delivered to venues in time for the shows. There was no trace of them as the night progressed, and Shane's friend's phone was not being answered. When he was discovered, the news was not good. He was returning to his hotel after a night of heavy drinking, and he had left Shane in the pub.

The fan who rescued the day, according to Nick Skouras, a session guitarist, was his nephew and godson Spiro. Nick had taken him to see The Pogues in Seattle and had planned to accompany him to New Orleans, but he had to cancel at the last minute. So Spiro had flown off on his own, carrying the clothes Nick had packed for himself, and in the foyer of his hotel, he spotted Shane passed out on the floor. He grabbed out his phone and called his uncle, not knowing what else to do. Shane has been aided and even carried on stage in a drunken stupor throughout the years. Musicians and crew members who have worked with him throughout his career have been surprised by his capacity to perform after lengthy drug and alcohol binges. During the reunion days, however, the shambolic scene at Voodoo Fest was the exception, not the rule. Mark Addis accompanied The Pogues on over 200 gigs, but only remembers three or four that were a flop. Whatever state Shane was in, even with barely hours to go, he was able to get on stage and finish the act. One of the most difficult tasks was keeping Shane's entourage away from backstage areas, his hotel room, or wherever else he could be discovered before a show, especially when he performed in Ireland. According to Mark, these hangers-on were more interested in having some great stories to feast out on than on Shane meeting his tour obligations. Shane's natural tendency to go with the flow and avoid conflict at all costs made keeping them at bay much more difficult. During his UK or Irish tours, one of his most infamous hangers-on would stay in his room every night, paying for everything, according to Mark. 'He is a leech and has always been one. But the thing about Shane is that he hates saying "No" to anyone... There have been plots to get them out of the hotel over the years, but they always find a way back in. Shane can be ignorant when it comes to how they can improve themselves. He would constantly fall for it, despite being an extremely intelligent and educated man, since he simply enjoys companionship. He dislikes sitting alone. Even if he's having a conversation with you and has been sleeping for half an hour, having someone there is soothing. He's a lonely guy, you know.' Victoria says that Shane's unwavering commitment and forgiveness allow others to exploit him. 'He's loyal to a fault, so he'll be loyal in ways that cost him a lot of the time,' she says. 'Someone may harm him and he would never stop them. He always notices and names everything in his head. He doesn't say anything to them, but he thinks to himself, I know he's ripping me off, or I know he's doing that. It makes no difference to him; he forgives such things. He will forgive almost anything. He's a very accepting person. 'He may have a friend who is bothering him, and he may tell them to fuck off or shut up. But it doesn't mean he won't give them money or help them in whatever way they need it. It simply indicates he doesn't want them to bother him.' Dave Lally was one fan who had shown Shane tremendous kindness and loyalty after they became friends. He, like Shane, had grown up in London in an Irish family and was quite proud of his background. He'd met Shane at shows over the years, quietly spoken and reticent, and had won his trust and respect. Later, after Shane was rendered immobilised by his accident, he travelled to Ireland to care for him while Victoria was gone. On my excursions to Dublin, he was in excellent company, and we became good friends. We talked on the phone on a daily basis, and he was very supportive of this book, putting me in touch with people to interview and serving as a sounding board. He died on March 15, 2020, just than two weeks before his 34th birthday, at his home in north London. Dave had witnessed people manipulating Shane for their own purposes firsthand and believed Shane's tolerance was due to feelings he had about some of his own past behaviour. 'He knows who is wicked and when they are up to something, whether it's stealing money or using him for drugs or fame. He also understands that people he adores, such as myself, Paul, and Scruffy, are rooting for him. He is quite devoted. Long before my time, he was always surrounded by terrible individuals. Junkies, users, whatever you want to call them. Shane has always referred to himself as a scumbag, and he messes up. He's a drug addict who has defrauded and beaten others. He's done a lot of shit. I believe he surrounds himself with horrible people because he thinks to himself, "Well, I'm a scumbag, but at least I'm not like that." If he is constantly surrounded by wonderful people, he will feel terrible about himself. Shane is like that, and he takes things seriously. Whatever rock'n'roll persona he may have, he's a small boy at the heart of it all.'

According to Mark Addis, Shane is uneasy in his own company and is comforted by the presence of others. He has no desire for their approval or respect. He finds solace in the simple presence of someone else. A cleaner arrived at his hotel room during a Pogues reunion tour. Shane apologised for the state of the room, which was as unkempt as he was, and instead invited her to sit and talk. If Shane was writing new stuff, there was no trace of it being recorded. He would occasionally join together with other musicians when he wasn't singing his old songs with The Pogues or Sharon Shannon's Big Band. However, it was never a serious endeavour. Shane seemed satisfied to drift, recording old covers with local musicians, for a songwriter and artist of international renown whose devotees read like a Who's Who of rock'n'roll. When he left The Pogues, he had a clear concept of what he wanted to achieve next and had worked with other great musicians such as Nick Cave, Van Morrison, and Christy Moore. He appeared to be staring back into his musical past, misty-eyed. The Nipple Erectors fans were surprised when the band regrouped for a secret show at London's 100 Club on May 6, 2008. Shane O'Hooligan was back, yelling down the mike and exuding punk bravado with his ex-girlfriend Shanne Bradley, guitarist Gavin

'Fritz' Douglas, and drummer Eric 'Le Baton' Baconstrip. Eucalypta, Shanne's 15-year-old daughter, was in the audience and came up on stage at the end to sing 'Gabrielle' with Shane. The band reformed the next year at Philly Ryan's in Nenagh, at Shane's request. Shane walked onto the little stage wearing a trilby and an eye patch, and footage from the wild event showed him absolutely rat-arsed. At one point, he fell off the stage and had to be assisted back up. Behind the drum kit was Shane and Victoria's buddy Michael Cronin, who had achieved success in Ireland with his brother Johnny's band The Aftermath. 'We walked out to The Commons and Shane was watching Daniel O'Donnell on RTE and drinking point,' Johnny recalls of a memorable inebriated day. We kept drinking and headed to Philly Ryan's to watch a hurling match. We had a terrific time that day because a large portion of Shane's record collection was present. On seven-inch, he was playing "Love" by John Lennon and "Some Of Your Lovin" by Dusty Springfield. We played it four or five times. The Chieftains' 'The Year Of The French' 'had a great impact on him, and I recall him performing it. So we did this show, and Shane was a little tipsy from the jam-jar.' A week after the surprise performance in Tipperary, the band performed something even more surprising. They gathered at the Cronins' Drumlish, County Longford, studio to re-record some of their original tunes. 'The band was down for about two days waiting for him, and I thought, This isn't going to happen,' Michael recounts. Shane did, however, come on the third day. One studio session in which Shane participated, and which saw the light of day, was a cover of Screamin' Jay Hawkins' "I

Put A Spell On You". Following the earthquake that struck Haiti on January 12, 2010, proceeds from Shane MacGowan & Friends' song were donated to the Dublin-based organisation Concern Worldwide. Shane came to the London studio with Victoria, joining a lineup that included Chrissie Hynde, Johnny Depp, Paloma Faith, and former Sex Pistols bassist Glen Matlock. 'When I got down there, Bobby Gillespie, Nick Cave, and Shane, and some other people started showing up,' Glen says. Later on, Mick Jones arrived and played with the fire extinguisher. They'd already recorded the music, so they tried their hand at singing, which I did, and Mick Jones took over the production for a while. Shane was sleeping on the sofa when the film crew arrived to shoot the video, and he suddenly awoke and said something cool. 'Chrissie Hynde came in and we were doing "I Put A Spell On You," which everyone thinks they know a little bit, and Chrissie was singing it completely incorrectly. Not out of tune, but there was a section where the verse came in and she sang it in time but twice as fast. I looked at Nick Cave, who looked at me and Shane, and we drew straws to see who would inform her. We were watching through the glass when Nick lost and had to leave. It was amusing.' The single did not chart because it was overshadowed by two other songs made for the Haitian appeal. Channel 4 News, on the other hand, was invited to the recording session and interviewed both Shane and Victoria. 'It just came to me as a great alternative to what Simon Cowell is doing, as an option for Haiti,' she said. 'I thought it seemed like a wonderful idea, and I felt he [Shane] would do it brilliantly, and I thought Nick would do it brilliantly.' When asked if the song was acceptable given its voodoo links, Shane responded, "Casting a spell on you doesn't mean a bad spell, it's casting a spell on you because I love you."

Shane's recording session was unusual. While Van Morrison and Elvis Costello had continued to write and release new work, Shane had gone thirteen years without producing anything. However, by the end of 2010, there were indicators that his songwriting hiatus was coming to an end. When Shane left Dublin for the comfort of Lanzarote to record with a new band, it was the coldest December since records began. They had rented some bungalows and planned to spend four weeks on the island writing and recording an album. The Shane Gang included drummer Paul Byrne of Celtic rock band In Tua Nua, bassist Jack Dublin, and Shane's old whistle buddy Joey Cashman. They'd played a few unplanned shows in Ireland, beginning at The Summit Inn in Howth, and Shane was upbeat about the new lineup.

In the end, there was no recording at all. Shane and a few friends, including Paul Ronan, headed out to the Canaries for a vacation. The Shane Gang did appear on the bill for Vince Power's London Feis Festival the following summer at Finsbury Park, however film footage of their concert shows them playing Pogues tunes 'Sayonara' and 'London Girl' rather than new material. Shane spent the rest of 2011 touring with The Pogues and as a Jools Holland tour guest. The Shane Gang vanished swiftly. Shane returned to Drumlish in 2012 to record a remake of 'The Rocky Road To Dublin' by The Dubliners with The Aftermath and others. The song 'The Rockier Road To Poland' was released to commemorate Ireland's qualification for Euro 2012 in Poland and Ukraine, the country's first qualification in twenty-four years. The entire profit was donated to the homeless charity Simon Communities of Ireland. It was the Cronins' idea to undertake a playful remix of the song, and they wanted Shane to be a part of it. Following an early recording, they called in others to finish the tune, including Father Ted comedic actor Joe Rooney, and a video was shot at the National Wax Museum in Dublin. What they didn't realise was that The Dubliners were recording the official anthem, 'The Rocky Road To Poland,' with Irish squad members.

On October 8, 2013, there was some bad news. Six years after being diagnosed with esophageal cancer, Philip Chevron died. He was only 56 years old. Not only did his former bandmates from The Radiators From Space and The Pogues mourn his death, but the entire Irish music world did. His final public performance had been during a testimonial event at Dublin's Olympia Theatre that summer. The event featured Shane and other members of the band, as well as notable Irish musicians such as Paul Brady, Mary Coughlan, Hothouse Flowers, Camille O'Sullivan, and playwrights Patrick McCabe and Joseph O'Connor. The Pogues sang Philip's song 'Thousands Are Sailing' beautifully. The evening was planned by Philip, who recruited Game of Thrones and Peaky Blinders actor Aidan Gillen to compare it. 'We had some mutual acquaintances, and he knew I was a fan of the Radiators,' Aidan explains. 'I'd never MC'd a night like that before, and I was nervous as anyone would be,' she says. I'm not sure how emotional Shane was. I believe that on nights like those, or any night, you sing the song.' Shane confirmed The Pogues' demise less than a year later. They'd grown tired of one other again, like they had in 1991, and Shane had had enough. On August 10, 2014, they performed their final gig at the Festival Fête du Bruit in Landerneau, France. 'I only wanted to do one gig to get out of a jam,' Shane explained to Uncut. 'I didn't plan for it to last this long. No, this is the end. This is the final year.' Shane was back in Ireland, working on a new record with Johnny and Michael Cronin at their recommendation. Even better, he'd grabbed up his pen again. 'I've composed a couple tunes,' he admitted. 'But I've been having a mental block.' The interviewer inquired as to whether Shane faced the same issue as Jerry Dammers of The Specials, who stated that it was difficult to surpass 'Ghost Town' when asked why he hadn't published a new song in thirty years. Shane responded, 'What, he thinks it's difficult to top "Ghost Town"? "Fairytale Of New York" must be surpassed. It doesn't frighten me! I'm already working on fresh material. You'll be notified when it's ready.' Shane's composing muse had returned, according to the Cronins, and there were fifteen 'classic MacGowan' songs ready for an album. 'Come Out, Ye Black And Tans,' the Irish rebel song by Dominic Behan, and old traditionals 'Wild Mountain Thyme' and 'Raggle Taggle Gypsy' were also being worked on during the sessions in Dublin. Shane appreciated the experience, but it was another false dawn, followed by an incident that would halt more than just his creativity. Shane has been in and out of the hospital like a 'yo-yo' throughout the years, breaking arms, legs, his pelvis, and hips. He had always healed, but when he collapsed in Dublin during the summer of 2015, the injuries he received would have long-term consequences for his quality of life. On Christmas Eve, he was still on crutches and attended a charity busking event in the city, accompanied on either side by Victoria and her nephew Olan. He would eventually require the use of a wheelchair to get about, and he is still unable to walk six years later. According to media sources, the fall occurred outside the recording studio. It actually happened as the Cronins dropped him off at the property he and Victoria were renting in Sandymount at the time. 'He got out of the van and sent me around for his bottle, and he simply dropped down on the pavement,' Michael explains. That's exactly what occurred.' Shane and the Cronins did get to record the official song when Ireland qualified for the UEFA European Championships again in 2016. 'Je t'aime Irelande' combined the Irish band A House's 'Endless Art' with Jane Birkin and Serge Gainsbourg's risqué duet, naming great Irish players and other national heroes. Shane performed 'Streams Of Whiskey' with Johnny and Michael at Ronnie Scott's in Soho for a spectacular charity event that year. The Hoping Foundation, which helps Palestinian refugee children, celebrated its tenth anniversary with the fundraiser. Van Morrison, Chrissie Hynde, Kate Moss, Noel Gallagher, Jools Holland, and Rob Brydon were also on the bill at the famed jazz club, which was also attended by Naomi Campbell, Bill Nighy, and Monica Lewinski. Shane stood with the help of a stick and appeared to be in pain. Shane's songwriting has always been a spontaneous process. When he first joined The Pogues, he would leave Victoria and his pals in the pub and go home to write when an idea struck him. Shane found it very frustrating that the well from which some of pop's finest storytelling had been taken had dried up. 'I spoke with Nick Cave about it, and he says he goes down to his desk on time every day and works and works. He'll write what he considers garbage and discard it all until he discovers something that appears to work. But Shane has never done something like that. He just gets it all, it comes through, he hears the music, and the words come. He sometimes thinks they're coming from a dead person or another being. So having that feeling that it wasn't going through meant he was shut off from his channel.' Shane's inability to get out and about has also kept him away from the experiences that inspired him, according to Victoria: 'A lot of the stuff came from socialising, so he'd be sitting there, listening to you, but not in the way you might assume. He could be listening for an idea, a couple of phrases, or something that could end up in a song. Because a lot of this occurs all the time, socialising was included in the study. 'I don't consider the block to be a bad thing. I believe he regards it negatively, but I believe it is not. I believe it is more about him questioning who he is without being the performance. "If I'm just me, who's that?" rather than "Who am I as Shane MacGowan?" 'People often talk about his being pissed,' Dave Lally noted, 'but Shane was hard-working.'He'd go home and turn on the TV or radio. He'd have someone in the room talking to him, and he'd be reading a couple books. He'd be doing all of this while also creating a song. He was still at work. Drink and drugs are involved, and the more popular you get, the more of them you will encounter. You require it. People say he blagged it, but Shane worked his bollocks off and no longer has them. 'He has nothing to inspire him at all.' Julien Temple comments on Shane's self-destructive lifestyle and the physical situation he currently finds himself in: 'Obviously, what he has done has taken its toll. It's what caused him to collapse. It's a way of life that will have implications, and it's a cautionary tale on one level. Do you have to go that dark and far into losing yourself to create anything as powerful as his body of work, or not? He raises a significant question. Did he need to be that tense and messed up all of the time? He boasts that he writes better when he's screwed up, which may be true.'

The crew gathered around their acclaimed patient and clapped when the gruelling operation was accomplished. They applauded again when he bit into an apple to put his new teeth to the test. When he saw himself in the mirror for the first time, he seemed satisfied. Despite his protests that he didn't want a sparkling Hollywood smile, he later had them changed with a whiter pair. Aside from aesthetic concerns, there was one thing neither he nor his dentist could control: how he sounded. 'When Shane had some teeth to work with, he recorded most of his outstanding masterpieces,' said Dr Mulrooney. 'Everyone's wondering how this will affect his voice. The tongue is a finely tuned muscle that moves precisely. We've essentially returned his instrument, and the process will continue.' Shane has defied all forecasts of his demise, outliving so many of those close to him.

Dave Jordan, Charlie MacLennan, Tommy McManamon, Joe Strummer, Kirsty MacColl, and Philip Chevron were all tragically killed when they were young. Frank Murray, 66, joined that list shortly before Christmas in 2016 after suffering a suspected heart attack. But it wasn't until the new year that Shane got the most shocking news of all. Therese had gone to Mass in Nenagh, as she did every Sunday, and was driving home when her car veered off the road and collided with a wall. There were no other vehicles involved, and it was suspected that she had suffered a heart arrest while driving. Shane's mother had been the first person to die on Irish roads in 2017 at three o'clock in the afternoon on New Year's Day. Philly Ryan, the town undertaker, had received a sombre call from the garda. He drove to the Silvermines Road location and began making preparations. He had been close to the family and had become fond of Therese as a result of his friendship with Shane. He also understood better than others the devastation her death would have on them all. Victoria had been informed of the news before Shane and was unsure how to break it to him. 'I was completely stunned,' she added. 'I bawled my eyes out, wondering how I was going to tell him? I couldn't think of anything to say to him. It took at least an hour for me to utter it. He didn't believe it at first. "No, that couldn't have happened," he said. "Not at all." Then he started thinking.' Therese was 87 years old. She had not been ill, and her death came as a complete surprise in the little town where she was well-known and liked. She and Maurice had celebrated their 60th wedding anniversary the previous August with a banquet at the Abbey Court hotel in Nenagh. Her relatives and friends had returned months later for her wake. Shane cut a fragile figure when he arrived in a wheelchair for the funeral service at Our Lady of Lourdes church in Silvermines, which was held precisely a week after the accident. His face was etched with sorrow, his pallor accentuated by his dark shades. Photographs published online and in the next day's newspaper showed him distraught. Siobhan and her husband Anthony led the pallbearers as the casket was carried into the packed church. Siobhan, like Shane, was extremely close to her mother, and her death had come as a horrible shock. She spoke of Therese's upbringing in Carney Commons, a little hamlet that produced 'giant characters' in her eulogy. The Lynches' house was well-known in the neighborhood for its "open door, hospitality, and generosity of spirit." With all the music and dancing, there would be sparks flying off the floor' in the cottage, but it was also a very spiritual place', filled with friendliness and where tears flowed easily. Siobhan described These as strikingly attractive and extroverted' when she and Maurice first met in Dublin. When she saw Maurice wasn't paying attention to her, she "set out to dazzle him - and dazzle him she did."

'Our parents were the best parents in the world,' Siobhan remarked. 'They instilled in us a fierce feeling of individualism, the ability to question and think for ourselves. My mother nurtured and lavished us with affection till the day she died. Everyone who knew her spoke highly of her grace. It was actual grace - a grace of the spirit - not merely elegance of movement or style. She had an open heart, a great compassion, and wisdom, which she shared with everyone she met. Many people who have written to us have mentioned her elegance and grace, but also her amazing sense of humour and fun. She was full of childlike wonder and a wise mind. With her amazing energy, she imparted advice, shared joy, and touched many lives. People felt more fortunate to have known her. 'The mark of a well-lived life.' Father Brendan Maloney, the parish priest, reminded the mourners that the day Therese died had been a "New Year's Day of sadness," but that it had been alleviated by "the joy of having Therese in your lives for so many years." He praised her singing talent, which she inherited from her family, and recalled how she had won accolades in her youth. 'She could have had a professional career since her singing was so amazing,' remarked many. She passed on her international stardom to Shane, and of course, Siobhan, you learned to write.'

Mundy was one among many who came to pay their respects. He'd seen her with Shane and been impressed by how close they were. 'I believe Shane was just turned upside down,' the musician and vocalist says. 'He appeared depressed and as if he hadn't slept in a long time. His mother used to attend Sharon Shannon shows. She would accompany Siobhan if we were playing in County Clare, which is close to Tipperary. They'd sit there, sharing their stockpile of booze and cigarettes. They wouldn't drink it all, but it was as if they were thinking, "What's the point of going up and down to the bar all evening when we're going to be here?" It felt like I was in an old Irish kitchen. They'd talk, and she'd tell him about him when he was a kid. He used to be quite polite around her. It was cute to behold, and not many people would get to witness it."His mother's death, I believe, hurt his heart severely. I met her once in Terryglass, Tipperary, with his sister. I believe he [Shane] had done physio or been in a clinic to recover from his fall, and he hadn't drunk in a long time. "If you meet him, don't encourage him," she said. He's doing fantastic." That was not long before she passed away.'

Shane's 60th birthday and contribution to Irish music were celebrated at Dublin's National Concert Hall, which was packed. A superb lineup of musicians had been assembled to pay tribute, but now it was Shane's turn. Shane appeared through a sea of cellphones and raised palms, pushed in his wheelchair by Victoria. Nick Cave greeted him on stage and sat beside him to sing "Summer In Siam" with him. A hush fell as Shane sang the first lyrics, and those fortunate enough to have secured tickets for this special night at Dublin's National Concert Hall strained to hear his unmistakable voice. The inclusion of ex-Pogues members Jem, Spider, Terry, and Cait in the band assembled for the occasion further added to the sadness of the event.

Shane sang well, and as the group's final record with him neared its conclusion, Nick wished him a happy birthday and lent over to embrace his long-time friend. He took his bow and left Shane to perform, with the audience spontaneously singing "Happy Birthday." They then sang the chorus of the traditional folk song 'Wild Mountain Thyme' with him. 'Will you go, lassie, go, and we'll all go plucking wild mountain thyme, all around the flowering heather...' There were no dry eyes in the house.

'I just wanted to sing a song with Shane,' Nick says. "We had recorded "Wonderful World" together years before, so it felt natural to sing with an old buddy again. I have never felt such a real sense of ecstasy come from an audience in all my years of performance as when lovely Victoria escorted Shane on stage. Shane raised his glass to the audience and began his verse of "Summer In Siam" - that lovely ballad of spiritual acceptance and love - and the audience simply melted. The support he received from the audience and his fellow artists was astounding. It was an emotional time for all of us, and one I will never forget.'

The list of artists who filed out on stage for the evening's grand finale served as testimony to the breadth of Shane's appeal: Bono, Johnny Depp, Sinéad O'Connor, Bobby Gillespie of Primal Scream, Clem Burke from Blondie, Catatonia singer and radio presenter Cerys Matthews, Libertines co-frontman Carl Barat, Finbar Furey. There were several recognized figures in the audience as well, including film director Neil Jordan, actors Stephen Rae and Cillian Murphy, and Sinn Féin president Gerry Adams. They had come from far and wide to celebrate Shane's 60th birthday and to witness a significant honour conferred upon him.

'Ladies and gentlemen, this has been a very wonderful evening, a celebration of one of our finest writers,' said compere John Kelly, a writer and broadcaster. And, as you know, we could have filled this hall ten times over because we all hold Shane MacGowan in such high respect. However, there will be one more homage tonight. The National Concert Hall is at the very core of music in this country, a location where music in all its forms, regardless of genre, is cherished and performed. The lifetime achievement award is the greatest honour that this organisation can offer. So I'm thrilled to announce that Shane MacGowan will receive a special lifetime achievement award from the National Concert Hall tonight in appreciation of his distinctive contribution to the art of songwriting.'

The audience applauded as Ireland's president and National Concert Hall patron, Michael D. Higgins, presented Shane with his award, a harp sculpture. The outsider whose lyrics and music were once considered heresy by some in Ireland was now hailed as one of the country's most celebrated sons. Shane's journey has been exceptional by any standard. Gerry O'Boyle came up with the idea to conduct an evening in Shane's honour after Therese died, and months of planning went into the event, which took place on January 15, 2018. 'Gerry has been such a wonderful friend to Shane,' Ann Scanlon says. 'He truly looks out for him, and Gerry was the one who organised his birthday show. You don't think you'll say "the greatest night of my life" when you're older, but there was never more love in a room. Gerry came up with that on such a gorgeous, brilliant night. "We should do something to cheer Shane up," he suggested, because his mother had died. Few composers with such a deeply entrenched Irish tradition have reached such a broad audience. Shane's fans come from punk, heavy rock, folk, pop, and every musical genre in between. Nick Cave, Paul Weller, Bono, Tom Waits, Van Morrison, Chrissie Hynde... The list goes on and on. His high regard demonstrates how deeply his timeless and poetic songs resonate with people. They, like Shane, are genuine. Bruce Springsteen is also awestruck by Shane's knack for language and the enduring quality of his songs. "He's the man, you know," he stated on The Late Late Show in October 2020. As I stated on my radio show, I genuinely believe that most of us will be forgotten in a hundred years, but Shane's music will be remembered and performed. It's just in the nature of things. So, he's the maestro for me, and I adore his work and the work he did with The Pogues."

Christy Moore is a long-time fan who believes Shane is among the greats of songwriting. 'More than any honours, Shane is adored... Occasionally pitied, but always adored. Most people think well of him, but some are frustrated by how his skills are believed to have been wasted. He has touched many people's hearts and emotions; he is a part of our culture, our underbelly, our soul, our crack. Only I can speak for myself. I consider him to be near the top of my list... Shane, Ewan MacColl, Bob Dylan, John Spillane, Wally Page, and Jimmy MacCarthy, to name a few. Shane's songbook gems were revisited for his birthday concert. Jesse Malin of New York, former Sex Pistol Glen Matlock, and Blondie drummer Clem Burke kicked off the night with songs like "That Woman's Got Me Drinking" and "Hot Dogs With Everything." A 'house band' then backed the various performers who took the stage to perform the songs Shane had carefully chosen for them. Johnny Depp joined Bono on guitar for 'A

Rainy Night In Soho,' and Bobby Gillespie gave 'A Pair Of Brown Eyes' the Primal Scream treatment. It fell to Glen Hansard and Lisa O'Neill to duet on 'Fairytale Of New York', while former Libertine Carl Barat drew everyone out of their seats with 'If I Should Fall From Grace With God'. Shane's frequent collaborator in Sharon Shannon's Big Band, Damien Dempsey, also contributed to the occasion. 'This is for all those people who claimed Shane wouldn't see 30,' he remarked, before leading a gallop through 'Bottle Of Smoke'.

Sinéad O'Connor was greeted enthusiastically by the audience, and as the applause subsided, she performed a hauntingly beautiful rendition of 'You're The One' (written by Shane and Michael Kamen), accompanied solely by piano and flugelhorn. The evening's emotions had been heightened by the unexpected death of Dolores O'Riordan earlier that day. The Cranberries singer, 46, was discovered dead in her hotel toilet. A heartbreaking conclusion to a turbulent existence. When John Kelly introduced Cerys Matthews to reprise 'The Broad Majestic Shannon,' he dedicated it to Dolores, much to the surprise of some in the crowd who had not received the news.

Shane also chose songs written by others. Terry Woods played 'Streets Of Sorrow,' which transitioned into Shane's 'Birmingham Six,' as it did on the record. Imelda May collaborated with Finbar Furey on the evergreen 'When You Were Sweet Sixteen,' which earned The Fureys and Davey Arthur an unexpected UK hit in 1981.

Finbar also delivered one of the night's most moving performances when he sang 'Kitty,' a ballad about a Fenian saying goodbye to his sweetheart from his prison cell. It struck a chord with Shane, who had learned it as a child from his mother. Shane was videotaped performing it in a bar for the BBC's 1997 documentary, The Great Hunger: The Life and Songs of Shane MacGowan, and Therese sang it for the camera during her interview.

Shane and Victoria were asked if they had a favourite performance when they appeared on The Ray D'Arcy Show on RTE Radio 1 a few days later. Victoria remarked that he couldn't have a favourite, but Shane responded, 'If pressed, I would pick Finbar.'

'I thought that was really generous of him,' Finbar says. 'It was lovely, and I thanked him profusely. When I got his rendition of the song, I wanted to do it exactly as he would. But I'm not Shane MacGowan. I'm Finbar Furey, and I performed it the way I felt it, and he got it, which I thought was wonderful. Myself and Peter Eades only had a guitar and a cuatro between us. It's a lovely song, and I felt every word of it.' Finbar recalls Shane's adoration that night, "All it was short of putting a crown on his head, they love him so much." Even with the heavyweights, the perfectionists, they'd have to admit defeat and say, "Yeah, you're right." You can't deny him; he's incredible, and I'll fight for him any day of the week."

Brendan Fitzpatrick, who watched the concert on a monitor backstage with Shane, said Finbar's rendition of 'Kitty' hit him hard. 'I remember sitting in the dressing room with Shane, and Finbar

Furey was playing "Kitty," and I could see there was a moment when a few tears began to flow because Shane was thinking about his mother,' Brendan recalls. 'It was a very touching moment in the concert for him, and he later said it was one of his favourite songs of the night. Even though it was a great celebration night for him, he couldn't help but think of his mother, who wasn't there to witness it. She had supported him throughout his career. I wrapped my arm around him and hugged him because I knew precisely where he was.'

The event left an indelible effect on fan and actor Cillian Murphy, well known for his role as Tommy Shelby in the BBC drama Peaky Blinders. 'I think that evening ranks as one of the great musical occasions of my life,' he recalls. 'There was such a buzz in the air that evening. The entire audience was such a devoted fan base, and to have that calibre and range of musicians, from original Pogues like Cait O'Riordan to Sinéad O'Connor to Nick Cave to Bono to Glen Hansard to Glen Matlock to Damien Dempsey to the president of Ireland himself, and a slew of others, all presided over with such calm and good nature by John Kelly, was a dream come true. It was a lovely evening that I'll never forget.' Following that, the festivities continued in an upstairs area, with people taking turns performing a song. 'Mundy and Glen both sang, and me and Steve Wickham played,' Sharon Shannon explains. 'At one point, Glen began calling Bono up, and I knew he was down in the far back corner with Johnny Depp, and there was no moving him. Finally, the Concert Hall called time, and we were all fucked.' Shane's towering legacy was recognized at the music industry's prestigious Ivor Novello Awards in London, just months after being honoured in Ireland. The British Academy for Songwriters, Composers, and Authors (BASCA) has presented the awards every year since 1956, and they symbolise peer acknowledgment for remarkable performance in classical, jazz, screen composing, and songwriting. Shane's inspiration award citation stated that he not only inspired bands like the Dropkick Murphys and The Libertines, who followed in The Pogues' boisterous wake, but also iconic people like Joe Strummer and Tom Waits, whose careers before his own. 'Ever since MacGowan emerged from the punk scene (his band The Nipple Erectors were a staunch support act during punk's initial wave), the raw reality of his music has been clear to anyone who has heard it, whether the songs date from his time with The Pogues or his solo career,' it read. After all, this is the man who, with the most cherished festive single of all time, "Fairytale Of New York," brought melancholy sincerity into the kitschy world of the Christmas song. A man who can perform wild-eyed party songs ("Fiesta", "Sally MacLennane") as well as sad-eyed, wistful ballads ("A Rainy Night In Soho", "A Pair Of Brown Eyes") equally well. And a man who deserves to be remembered for far more than his well-documented fondness for alcohol.' Former Stiff boss Dave Robinson was among those there at the Grosvenor House hotel to honour Shane, 34 years after seeing The Pogues at The Pindar of Wakefield and deciding to sign them. Shane was joined on stage by Gerry O'Boyle and Victoria for the presentation, which was given by actor Aidan Gillen. 'I was thrilled that Shane had asked me to present it and extremely happy that he was getting fair respect for his music since Shane is a songwriter above all else,' recalls Aidan. 'He's a frontman, a vocalist, but most importantly - and this is becoming increasingly clear - he's a songwriter, the likes of whom don't come along very often. I'd written a couple early copies of what I was going to say on the day, and it looked like the most difficult part would be removing superlatives and comparisons to Nick Cave, Bob Dylan, or anybody; the other best songwriters around who've all previously praised Shane.' Aidan's girlfriend Camille O'Sullivan was also in attendance to see Shane honoured. She has toured with The Pogues and sung the parts of 'Fairytale Of New York' that Kirsty MacColl imprinted on mainstream culture. She had just been given an hour's notice the first time she was asked to sing the song. Therese MacGowan was unable to perform with Shane at Dublin's Olympia venue, so Victoria called Camille, who was at a friend's house, and dashed to the venue. 'Like everyone else, I knew the song, but I realised I didn't know it well enough,' Camille explained. 'I had someone print off the lyrics, and I cycled down to Dame Street, trying to understand them on the way. I initially met Shane while singing with him onstage. It was frightening. His mother typically sang it, but she was unable to do so that night. It was the most crazy first meeting I'd ever had with somebody.' Aidan has made friends with Shane and Victoria and visits their Dublin flat. He's seen westerns and horror movies with Shane and enjoyed a few beers with him, so much so that he couldn't put his shoes back on when it was time to leave. When asked about the man he is still getting to know, Aidan says, 'There's a lot I don't know about him yet. But if I had to pick some characteristics, I'd say: fast, cool, witty, real, and bashful.' As an Irish person living in London, the Dublin-born actor was among those to whom Shane's lyrics spoke so directly. Aidan explains: 'Having gone to London as a teenager and stayed for twenty years, I was fully acquainted with the entire London Irish culture that The Pogues could only have emerged from. It appears to be an easy enough scene to explain, but it is not. Being an outsider in both countries, yet enjoying the best of both worlds and making a lot of noise if you wanted to. It's a distinct and potent niche to be in... the streets of King's Cross, Camden, Kilburn, and Soho that I traversed ceaselessly since the late 1980s. A lot of the time, it was a lonely scenario. But I wanted to be an actor, and those songs often kept me sane.' Shane's lyrics are raw and emotional. Death, violence, and guilt are prominent themes, and broken characters populate shady alleys and taverns. It's no surprise that his music has captivated so many celebrities, including Johnny Depp, Matt Dillon, Matthew McConaughey, Robert De Niro, and Sean Penn. Some were in bands themselves, and their music was influenced by The Pogues.

When Cillian Murphy was growing up in County Cork, he played in a band with his brother Páidi. His parents accompanied him and his siblings to sessions where traditional Irish music was played. But it was The Pogues that popularised Irish music. 'After school, the drummer in our band and one of my longest friends, Bob Jackson, asked me to his gaff and turned up Rum Sodomy & The Lash incredibly loud in his garage,' recalls Cillian. 'All of a sudden, this synchronicity between punk and traditional music exploded in my ears. It was unlike anything I'd ever heard - and it made perfect sense. Shane's lyrics, the manner he sung them, and the wildness of the playing made him an immediate hero for all youngsters.'

Songs about whiskey and Soho's neon-lit streets were mythical to a youngster growing up in rural Ireland, evoking a world that felt imaginary rather than real. 'His songs feel like they've been passed down through the generations,' Cillian explains. 'Each one feels like it might be a story. The poetry of the lyrics juxtaposed against the ferocity and abandon of the performance was probably what drew me in at first. The way the songs were violent and sweet, frequently in the same song, "A Pair Of Brown Eyes" for example. The how the lyrics become clearer with each listen. They're full of historical and literary allusions that were, and probably still are, completely beyond me at the time!'

While Shane's pen hasn't produced songs with such everlasting resonance in more than two decades, his impact on other artists and performers hasn't lessened. The brutal truth of Shane's words and the ferocity of The Pogues may be heard from Boston-based punks the Dropkick Murphys and Irish American ensemble Flogging Molly to The Libertines and The Decemberists. Contemporary musicians born long after Rum Sodomy & The Lash and If I Should Fall From Grace With God continue to be inspired by the tunes.

Joy Crookes, a singer from London, is 23 years old. Her Bangladeshi mother introduced her to Sufi music, while her father introduced her to The Dubliners and The Pogues. He also instilled in her the value of her Irish background from a young age. 'My dad used to say to me growing up, "I don't care about your English accent, the fact your skin is brown, and how you want to dress - you're Irish!" says the young artist, who has been nominated for a Brit Award in 2020. He used to make me recite Yeats with him before bed, send me to Irish dancing lessons (I got a D), and play me everything from Sinéad to Van and The Chieftains' rendition of Paddy Kavanagh's "Raglan Road." He was a fan of The Pogues, and their music permeated into my young bones.'

Joy shared a video of herself playing guitar and singing 'A Pair Of Brown Eyes' on YouTube when she was 15 years old. So, as she began to develop her own writing style, she considered how and why Shane's songs had such an impact on her.

'From Shane, I learned a lot about Ireland and Irish communication,' Joy explains. 'His voice and lyrics would always make me imagine a situation, whether it was "Summer In Siam" or "A Pair Of Brown Eyes." As I grew older, the lyrics became more meaningful to me; I felt like I could identify with them and, more significantly, I realised Shane was a storyteller. His vision is both broad and intimate, as if he were speaking directly to us, the offspring of Irish exiles.'

According to Shane's friend Ann Scanlon, he had always thought Irish music was cool, and his ambition to see other musicians passionately express their Irishness and delve into the country's poetic essence had been fully realised. 'When Shane was living in

The Boogaloo, he told me, "I'm going to set up this thing called 'Hip Eire' because we've always been hip," Ann says. 'As I understood it, his ambition was for all the young bands to take up the mantle, and in some ways, this has happened because we'd speak about people playing "Raglan Road" incredibly fast, and you've had Lankum, Lisa O'Neill, and people like that. Fontaines D.C., in my opinion, are the band that is truly doing it. Grian [Chatten] has that quality Shane has, that quiet sensitivity, that poet soul. He was born in England and has an Irish accent. "It feels nice to wear our Irishness on our sleeve because it's a voice that's been downtrodden," he remarked, and that's like Shane.

CHAPTER 6

A FURIOUS DEVOTION

The fact that Shane had gained such acclaim for his poetic and enduring compositions should not have taken anyone by surprise. But the news that broke in November 2018 made people's mouths drop. Shane and Victoria were finally marrying.

After Victoria shared a Facebook photo taken through the window of a plane with the enigmatic statement, 'Off on a covert mission,' rumours flew. The Irish Sun published an exclusive the next day, confirming the couple's marriage: 'Shane MacGowan will conclude the longest engagement in rock'n'roll history by finally marrying Victoria Mary Clarke this Monday,' it said. The wedding would take place in Copenhagen, Denmark, rather than his home Ireland. According to an unidentified acquaintance, it was to be a 'intimate occasion' with no celebrity guests.

Some close to the couple were as surprised as the rest of the world. After all, it had been eleven years since Victoria had flashed her engagement ring on The Pat Kenny Show, and they had split up multiple times since, with little public hint of a wedding. They had broken up again in the summer of 2016, and Shane had taken it personally. Maurice was so concerned about him that he called Paul Ronan and requested that he go to Ireland to be with Shane. Therese, ever the adoring mother, had stayed up all night with her kid. In the end, Victoria took him back, as she always did.

As the wedding date approached, Maurice was being treated at Dublin's Mater Private Hospital, and Siobhan was staying in a hotel so she could see him every day. Anthony, Siobhan's husband, was also travelling up and down from their home in Tipperary to encourage Siobhan and lift Maurice's spirits. Maurice's continued treatment prevented him and Siobhan from attending the wedding, but Shane went to see him and addressed his upcoming nuptials.

The original idea was to fly to the Bahamas, where their Hollywood A-list pal Johnny Depp would perform the ceremony. However, with Shane in a wheelchair, such a long flight was impossible, and Victoria's family would have to travel a significant distance. They instead chose a low-key civil ceremony in Copenhagen City Hall. Victoria clarified in her Sunday Independent column that there would be no flower girls, page boys, or matrons of honour. They weren't even going to exchange wedding rings.

So, thirty-two years after they first met and eleven years after they became engaged, why were they finally marrying? 'I proposed to him immediately after we met because it was a leap year, and he said he didn't want to get married,' Victoria explains. I don't recall proposing again for a long time, but he did after I dumped him. "No, let's get married," he said, and I said, "No, I've broken up with you now, and I've found someone else." That was obviously why he wanted to marry. So, when we reconnected, we both agreed that getting married was a fantastic idea. But once we were engaged, we didn't feel compelled to go through with it because neither of us wanted the hassle. Neither of us enjoys making a fuss; we prefer to shift it to someone else. So, with all that commotion and questions... Oh, God, so many questions, and so many individuals we don't even know... We couldn't do it because it was a nightmare.

'The notion of going to Copenhagen came from me because I reasoned that since we didn't know anyone in Copenhagen, we could just go there and no one would know. I could bring my sister as a witness, but if I bring my sister, I'll have to bring my mother... However, there are those people with whom we feel so at ease that we might as well be at home.'

Shane and Victoria married on Monday, November 26th, 2018. Victoria's parents, sister Vanessa, and other family and friends were there as witnesses. Despite reports that their famous friends would not be joining them, Johnny Depp flew in, ensuring that photos were circulated around the world. Victoria looked stunning in a stunning crimson Bella Freud gown with long sleeves and a floral headband. Shane wore a black trilby hat, a dark overcoat, with a shirt and tie.

After the couple tied the knot, Johnny and Michael Cronin sang 'A Rainy Night in Soho' to the couple and their guests, with Johnny Depp joining in. The Cronins had become close to the couple and were honoured to be asked to perform at the wedding. 'That morning, we were in the car with Shane and we were going on about songs from Veedon Fleece,' Johnny recalls. We began singing "Linden Arden Stole The Highlights," and Shane began telling me about Linden Arden. Also, on the way to his wedding, he was singing "If I

Fell," and it was amazing to see how happy he was to meet Victoria. It was simply a lovely moment. We returned to the Tivoli Gardens, which resembled a winter wonderland, for dinner before performing some songs. Because "Astral Weeks" is a favourite of Shane and Victoria, we played it with Johnny Depp. Shane didn't want to hear "A Rainy Night In Soho" because he had so many other amazing songs.'

Shane and Victoria flew home the next day as Mr. and Mrs. MacGowan. The scenic backdrop in the Danish capital, combined with friends who had travelled to celebrate with them, had created for a fantastic evening for Victoria. She was also taken aback by the effect it made on Shane.

'It was so much greater than I could have dreamed because it was like enchanting every minute,' Victoria says. 'I guess it was partially the setting because Tivoli Gardens is like something out of a fairy tale. It is the world's oldest fairground, but it looks like something out of a Disney movie. It's almost magical with the snow and Christmas trees. Then, of course, having Johnny [Depp] and the Cronins singing was breathtaking. It was a huge success. Shane was genuinely impacted by it, I believe, and he changed as a result. He genuinely softened, and I believe he felt more loved as a result.'

Shane smiles as he looks up. He is sitting in his favourite armchair and immediately begins nattering. He's in excellent shape, and this is the first time I've seen him penning ideas in a notebook. After landing in Dublin, Paul Ronan and I went directly to visit him. Shane is certainly pleased to see us in November 2018. The man I've come to know is uninterested in his own company. Even if the room is quiet, he wants to know that people are around, just as the bottle of white wine in front of him provides a soothing presence. I'm delighted we arrived. Shane has spent the most of his life surrounded by people. His natural shyness can still be seen in a busy environment or when meeting new individuals for the first time. He is not an extrovert and never asserts himself. He is most content when he is listening to other people's voices. Jem travels from London to see him on a regular basis, while Joey remains a consistent caller. Friends from Nenagh also stay in touch and fly to Dublin to see him.

Victoria adores him, and after everything they've been through, it's impossible to imagine him without her. He has become increasingly reliant on her and others since damaging his hip. Meanwhile, his physio, Paddy Pio O'Rourke, a Tipperary native, has been assisting him in regaining strength.

The Irish Sun published a photo showing them both, Shane standing with the help of rails, under the heading FAIRYTALE showing NEW WALK in April 2019. Paddy Pio discussed how he used music to motivate Shane to do his workouts and noted that he was making excellent progress. 'Since I began working with Shane, he has been incredibly determined to get back on his feet, and he's doing pretty well,' he explained. 'He's now a huge Post Malone fan!' During one of our first sessions, his [Post Malone's] song "Rockstar" came on through my playlist, and he couldn't stop giggling at parts of the lyrics. And now that he's discovered the rest of his music, we normally blast it as loud as we can, and Shane does his finest work.' Victoria was overjoyed at the effect Shane's trainer was having. 'I believe that psychology plays a significant role in getting people going when they have experienced mobility challenges. He's fantastic.'

Shane got to sing with his old buddy Chrissie Hynde in June 2019, which has been increasingly rare in recent years. When The Pretenders opened for Fleetwood Mac at the RDS in Dublin, they sang 'I Got You Babe,' and Chrissie spent time with him at his nearby house. Shane made a brief cameo at the Liverpool Feis the previous summer, leading the throng in a singalong of 'Dirty Old Town'.

I've only seen Shane a few times since his injury, and I'm curious how he's coping with the life he's been forced to live. I've seen a reluctance on his part to leave the flat, possibly because it requires too much work and he feels more at ease at home. 'I'm going to compel them [doctors] to do it,' he said one night as we talked. I'm off to the newspapers. They refuse to operate on my hip, leaving me unable to walk and jeopardising the rest of my life. I enjoy jogging, running, and kicking the snot out of anybody, including them! It's not a big danger, and I'd rather take it. I used to shatter everything and recover in a week. But nothing changed this time because they did nothing. Now I'm not sure what's going on. I have a 91-year-old uncle who knows his thing, and I'm going to go to him and ask him what kind of procedure I need. I don't mind if it's lengthy and complicated, but I don't see why it should be. It's only a fractured hip, but it's a big deal in this country because everyone is athletic, participates in GAA [Gaelic Athletic Association - promoting Gaelic sports], fights a lot, goes after ladies, and runs after males with spades in their hands, tsscchh... If necessary, I'll have it done in England. Who cares if you're in the hospital?'

Shane was treated at two private hospitals in Dublin after his fall, and his fractured pelvis healed. Several months later, he was returned home with the intention of having his hip operated on when his body was ready. But it never happened, and while his friends are saddened to see him unable to walk, some blame it on his refusal to prepare for surgery.

'When he was in the Mater Private, Mark [Addis] and I went to visit him,' says Terry Woods. They were detoxifying him, which was taking some time. They couldn't do it swiftly because his body couldn't handle it. "He should really go home," they said. We'll continue with the cleanse. He's also malnourished, and his body needs to be physically restored before we can perform surgery. His body would be unable to withstand an anaesthetic."'

According to Sinéad O'Connor, Shane has been hesitant to have hip surgery since he won't be able to access his medications (the illicit sort) while in the hospital, and his continuous use of them gives his expressed wish to get better a hollow ring. 'He doesn't want to live, otherwise he wouldn't be doing so many drugs,' Sinéad explains. 'Nobody doing those things wants to survive, whether it's a tramp on the street, a person in an apartment, or Shane. They wish to be undead, meaning neither dead nor living. He would be doing his physiotherapy to get up and walk if he wanted to survive. There is no reason he can't walk right now except that he gave up... I saw a man who had given up five years ago. His bed is facing his television and resembles a coffin. He has his alcohol on one side and his pills on the other. He has the remote and sits there all day...

'The quantity of garbage he's ingesting... If I took one of those Valiums, let alone using them to get out of bed in the morning and a ton of alcohol, I'd be in the hospital. You can die from it, and if he says he wants to live, he's lying. He isn't interested in living. I've watched a lot of TV shows over the years, particularly in Ireland, where everyone feels sorry for him and says, "Oh, poor Shane." If he could only get his act together." However, this is chocolate and vanilla.

'There are millions of people in the world of various types, and he is just as he should be. It is not for us to feel sorry for him, change him, or wish for him to be different. He is 60 years old and has made the decision to be who he is. So we must respect and adore him for it, as well as the fact that once he got his foot up his arse, he accepted it. He has been responsible in some ways ever since.'

One evening, we were discussing his health when Shane abruptly changed the subject. This is something he uses frequently, sometimes as an avoidance tactic and sometimes to redirect the conversation to one of his favourite topics. On this occasion, the subject is one that has consumed his thoughts since boyhood. The Unrest.

'I don't want to die right now. I don't want to die in any way. But the fact that other people squandered so much of their lives blowing up other people who wasted their lives, and the lack of retribution. They must compensate hundreds of people and their friends and relatives on both sides of the schism, which is absolutely messed up.' If you sit with Shane for any length of time, the subject of Northern Ireland will come up. For the majority of his life, he has been fascinated and afflicted by its painful fights, and it is a subject that can cause the passionate outbursts that have become a part of his personality. This is his safe haven. He understands everything there is to know about Irish history and is a fervent republican who considers former Sinn Féin president Gerry Adams as a personal friend.

Shane learned about his forefathers fighting for 'the cause' and how an entire division of Black and Tans were murdered and buried near the cottage while on vacation at The Commons. He was given a copy of Dan Breen's My Fight for Irish Freedom, which was described as "very violent and very graphic." Breen was a member of the IRA's third Tipperary Brigade and was involved in the ambush and killing of two RIC policemen, which is regarded as the start of the War of Independence. He was the first republican elected to the Free State Parliament, representing Tipperary for over thirty years.

Shane's 'furious love' to Ireland strengthened as he grew older, giving him the identity he never had growing up in England. His family's republican credentials became a keystone in his biography as he rose to popularity with The Pogues.

Despite the fact that neither The Pogues nor The Popes were overtly political, Shane has contributed to the rebel songbook. He sang in 'Skipping Rhymes' from The Crock Of Gold, 'We put a hood over his head/Then we shot the bastard dead/With a nick-nack, paddy-wack give a dog a bone/Send the stupid bastards home'. 'The nation's going to rise again,' the chorus repeated four times. The song 'Paddy Public Enemy No. 1' from the same album was inspired by the narrative of republican paramilitary Dominic 'Mad Dog' McGlinchey. After being dismissed from the IRA, he became chief of staff for the Irish National Liberation Army and was later killed.

The album's debut came just two months after the start of Northern Ireland's peace talks, which would result in the Good Friday Agreement. Shane did not shy away from expressing his republican views in promotional interviews. 'I believe it should happen now; the English should leave,' he remarked. 'We've had enough, they should let the Irish govern their own nation,' I say. I've long maintained that the Brits have no business being there. I believe in a republic, specifically a socialist republic.'

Shane had met Sinn Féin leader Gerry Adams that summer during the Féile an Phobail, the West Belfast Festival, which was organised in response to the Troubles and took place on and near the Falls

Road. In an interview with the RTE Guide, Shane stated he thought they had mutual respect' throughout their meeting. Gerry Adams continues to write to Shane, and the two have remained friends.

When Victoria began recording chats with him for her book A Drink with Shane MacGowan, this unexpected encounter with Adams was still fresh in his mind. When she asked him what it meant to him to be Irish, his response was stunning. 'The Pogues would not have existed if I hadn't been Irish,' he explained. 'To me, Ireland is everything. I've always felt bad for not laying down my life for Ireland, for not joining up. Probably wouldn't have helped the situation. But I was ashamed that I hadn't had the courage to join the IRA. And The Pogues were my way of getting over my guilt. And, looking back, I believe I made the right decision.'

It's unclear how the republican movement would have perceived someone who wore a Union Jack shirt in the same neighbourhoods where they were placing bombs. Shane's transformation from punk with a London accent to staunch Irish republican has sparked debate over the years. In his 1995 memoir, John Lydon stated, "Shane MacGowan used to come and see us play all the time." He'd be down in the front, completely pissed off in his Union Jack T-shirt. He switched it in for [an Irish] tricolour when he joined The Pogues.'

Julien Temple, who directed the 2020 documentary Crock of Gold: A Few Rounds with Shane MacGowan, was the first person to interview him in 1976, shooting him in the lift of a block of flats. He didn't see anything of his Irish heritage at the time, which would become crucial to his identity. "He was like Joe [Strummer]; he had a thick London street accent that was probably forced - the mockney style," Julien adds. 'But being a punk required you to be like that. It was all about burying your history and remaking yourself, which I believe suited Shane perfectly, as it did Joe and many other individuals... If you didn't know his name, there was no sign of Irishness. A lot of Irish people were very London at the time, and you wouldn't have realised he was Irish, and you certainly wouldn't have guessed he'd go on to do what he did.'

Siobhan, on the other hand, sees no conflict between his republican ideals and his punk dress. 'I do believe that the Union Jacks on the shredded punk shirts were a type of mocking and rebellion against the flag," she explains. 'I believe Shane wore it in that spirit.'

Another recurrent motif in Shane's biography, as he puts it, is violence, from his role as 'minister for torture' and his ties with Charlie Kray while at Westminster to those he left lying in a pool of blood years later. He was at his most impassioned when telling these anecdotes, in my opinion. I couldn't help but wonder how many of them were the result of his vivid imagination.

I asked him if he was worried as a teenager about hanging out with dangerous underworld types like Kray. 'Of course not,' he exclaimed. 'I come from a criminal family and a criminal race.' I request that he elaborate. 'The older ones were in the IRA, and the younger ones were still hanging out with the IRA and foot troops,' he explains.

'Was the Commons also used as a safehouse?' I ask.

'Yes, many years before my birth. My great-grandfather, who went to the house, was the local IRB, the Irish Republican Brotherhood - the Fenians, as they were known when he first started. They formed the IRA.'

Terry Woods' family was active in the 1916 insurrection, and he, like Shane, is well-versed in the turbulent history of Ireland. So Shane has always wanted to talk about it with him. 'Shane zeroes in on it,' says Terry. We used to have absurd conversations about it. But he believes a lot of this nonsense... When you examine the thread that runs through his life, all the alcohol and drugs he's consumed since a young age. So his thinking isn't clear in any way, shape, or form, and it wouldn't surprise me if he believes anything to be true.'

Shane has been living in a bubble, cut off from the rest of the world, for several years. He almost never looks at a computer. He does not have access to email. He has a phone next to him, but he doesn't use it since he prefers to watch TV. Gerry O'Boyle and Victoria, who have played a crucial part in keeping his reputation up after he left The Pogues, schedule and coordinate any public appearances.

Victoria has spent the last few years pursuing her dream of filming her relationship with Shane. She spent two years co-writing a script with her filmmaker friend Maeve Murphy and announced toward the end of 2019 that her spouse would be played by award-winning Dunkirk actor Barry Keoghan. Even more thrilling for fans was the fact that Shane was back in the studio working on the music.

'Most of those rock biopics are really from the rock star's point of view, so it's sort of exciting for me to have the opportunity to write about Shane, but from my point of view - and he hasn't seen any of it,' Victoria said in a TV interview. 'He hasn't seen the screenplay,' he says. "Can you just give me permission to do it without interfering?" I guess I asked, since I don't try to write the music, you know what I mean?'

When asked if the film will be a candid look at their relationship, Victoria said, 'Absolutely. "Look, make sure you put in all the violence, all the drugs, all the danger, and all that stuff," he did say. Don't make it schmaltzy or like a Hugh Grant flick."

Maeve met Shane and Victoria through Frank Murray at the end of the 1980s. He had backed Trouble And Strife, the theatre group she formed and co-wrote and acted in. She claims that the idea for the film came from a dream she had about Shane. He was in the same room as the actor who portrayed a prison officer in her 2001 film Silent Grace, and when she stepped in, she felt at ease. The next morning, she emailed Victoria. 'At first, I assumed it was just going to be about Shane,' Maeve explains. 'But after I started researching and talked with Victoria, I realised their love story was just a great story.'

According to Maeve, there is a mystery about Shane and Victoria as a pair that 'fascinates and touches' and makes their narrative interesting. The turbulent nature of their relationship is fundamental to its big-screen appeal, as the script explores both their bad and good days as a couple. 'It's appealing because it's a cinematically exciting edgy love,' explains Maeve. 'At times wild and exhilarating, at times dangerous and doomed. I love how, when it's doomed, we can't see how it could ever work...'

Victoria's love of attention and celebrity has always clashed with Shane's utter disinterest. He maintains an exceedingly quiet life, with only a few close pals. Joey Cashman is larger-than-life, the ideal foil for a shy man who tells his story via music. If Shane isn't in the mood to converse, Joey is just as likely as anyone else to entice him. But most of the time, Shane is happiest when he's watching a gangster movie with a friend by his side.

'Shane just wants affection and company,' Dave Lally remarked. When I'd bring him a gift, he'd become all thrilled and say, "What, for me?" He'd be in shock and would hide it in case it went missing. When we meet up after not seeing each other in a while, he usually asks about my mother. He despises negative news and will take it personally if I tell she hasn't been feeling well. Shane is extremely sensitive... I'm usually quiet, and when I'm with him, we'll relax and watch a movie together. We may merely say a few words in the first hour. He simply desires my presence; he desires companionship. He'll fall asleep, and when he wakes up, he'll have no idea where he is or who is in the room. He'll see me and say nothing before returning to his television. But I'm present.'He continues to live his life in the same manner. Just the TV and a few pounds to get him through the day of drinking and smoking. That is all Shane desires.

He has a very simple life, and I believe all he wants is to be surrounded by his friends and loved ones.'

Shane, according to Victoria, has never been able to cope with awful news stories, especially when they involve individuals in pain. 'I think he feels linked to people, so if anything horrible happens to someone, he feels it,' she explains. Not just those he knows, but the First World War, the Second World War, and Vietnam - he takes them all extremely seriously. Even though they occurred in the past, they are very real to him, and those people are real people who are suffering, dying, and being tormented. To him, it's not as if it occurred to someone else; it happened to a person, a human being. He's a good dude.'

If Shane has a violent side, it is exhibited in an explosive temper, as many of those who have tried to interview him can attest. Victoria claims he despises questions and has never been comfortable discussing his music or career. In such instances, he may adopt an angry and cutting tone. Friends have also found themselves on the receiving end of his harsh tongue throughout the years. Shane, on the other hand, is not cruel and feels bad when he knows he has upset someone he loves about.

'I was around at his flat and he offended me,' Paul Ronan recalls. He was being obnoxious, as Shane can be at times, and I recall storming out and telling him, "You can just go fuck yourself."

'I just got home, and when I opened the door, the phone rang, and it was Shane. "Look, Paul, I apologise. "Can we go down Le

Mercury?" asked the waiter, referring to a French restaurant on Upper Street in Islington. "I'll buy you a meal, and we'll talk over a few drinks." I'll come over and get you a cab."

'"No," I answered. I'll either come over to you or meet you down there.""Get yourself a cab," he continued, "and I'll look after it." That demonstrates Shane. He dislikes disturbing individuals who are close to him. He may scoff, but if he believes he has overstepped the mark or been unpleasant, he becomes quite sorry.'

During a drinking session in Nenagh one night, Shane began taunting Dave Lally and referring to him as a 'West Brit' - an Irish guy with a more British attitude - despite the fact that he was born in the UK. Nothing was said after that, and Dave had not ruminated on it. Shane brought it up again several years later. 'He turned around and said, "I'm sorry about upsetting you that time," Dave said.

"What time?" I inquired.

'"When I was taking the piss in Nenagh and calling you a West Brit," he says. I wasn't serious."

'"Shane, forget about it," I said. If I was upset about it, I wouldn't be here."

'"Well, I was only joking, I didn't mean it," he explained. I apologise."'

One day, Paul and I were in a Dublin pub with Shane when a fan approached us and asked who I was. I introduced myself as Shane's friend.

'You're not one of my friends,' Shane remarked, glancing at me.

'All right, you're correct. 'I'm not one of your friends,' I explained.

After a few seconds, Shane said, 'Actually, you are a friend of mine.'

Shane spends the entire day with a bottle of white wine and a glass in front of him. He will occasionally fill his glass to the brim and leave it for half an hour or more without drinking a drop. As one bottle is emptied, another is opened, and it is within his grasp even when he goes to bed.

For almost forty years, alcohol has been his steady companion. Long before he was downing bottles of whiskey on stage with The Pogues or pints of gin for martinis in the Popes years, his Cromer Street flat was a sea of empty bottles. When he performed with Sharon Shannon's band, he kept his wine on a little table beside his microphone stand, always within reach. Even as he accepted his top honours in 2018, he held a drink. Shane, on the other hand, has abstained from alcohol for six months. That dry stretch started in the middle of 2016, when he was readmitted to the hospital with agonising hip pain and pneumonia. Shane spent several months in his secluded room without touching a drop after his doctors prescribed a thorough detox. Even when he came home, he didn't drink. 'This is the longest Shane has been sober since we met, and we're getting along great,' Victoria exclaimed. I never imagined Shane could be joyful and sober at the same time.'

Shane has always maintained his freedom to drink, telling journalists that what he did was none of their business. Over the years, Siobhan, Victoria, and others have asked him to stop. They have come to accept, however, that when it comes to his lifestyle, he will only listen to one voice. His personality. 'I have tried over the years to give him wake-up calls, but you might rouse him up for five minutes,' Siobhan adds. It's not going to last.'

The fact that he is still alive after decades of self-abuse appears to have infused him with the conviction that, whatever dependencies he may have, he is not completely under their control. Although his limits dwarf those of most people, he has always known how to stay inside them. 'When I say you've had enough, you've had enough,' he snarled at a drunken woman who joined his party in a London hotel.

'One drink can set you up to be an alcoholic,' says Shane. 'You have one in the morning and one in the afternoon, and you try to remember it. That's the only way to stay sober for any length of time. When you are withdrawing from alcohol, you cannot sleep, and alcohol is a potent drug. It's the worst of the bunch. It makes you sick if you don't have it, and you don't enjoy it after a few glasses. Nobody drinks for the sake of the taste. I drink to get a fucking high. I drink slowly and don't drink as much as I used to. 'I require it, but I am not an alcoholic.'

When asked if she believes Shane is an alcoholic, Victoria responds, 'He probably isn't. I believe if they gave him a different drug and told him, "This drug is going to actually do the same thing," he would accept it. It's whichever medicine will make him feel normal. I believe he romanticism drinking in the same way that hard men and Irish men drink, and if you can't drink, there's something wrong with you.'

Over the years, Victoria has witnessed peaks and valleys in his drinking. She claims that when The Pogues achieved prominence and the urge to tour grew, his alcohol use skyrocketed. 'He used to get extremely anxious on tour, and that's when he used to drink a lot,' she says. It was quite difficult for him. I recall one day while we were driving about Dublin in my car, I saw he didn't have anything to drink. 'That's extremely strange, he usually has a drink,' I thought. When I told him, he replied, "Yeah, but I've got nothing to worry about." He wasn't stressed because we weren't on tour and he wasn't required to be anyplace or do anything. So I believe he feels a lot of pressure, even if it's just pressure to go anywhere.'He drinks to get high. When we first met, I used to drink a lot more than him, which surprised him. I didn't drink to get high. I drank to become wasted, which he thought was a little excessive. He'd say, "Oh, why are you drinking so much?" and drink a white wine spritzer as I drank a double or triple whiskey. So, when The Pogues took off, I observed a difference, and when he was under pressure, he completely transformed. He grew anxious and couldn't deal with the guilt of not accomplishing what they needed him to do, as well as the obligation of all these people whose jobs were at stake. He couldn't just walk away. It was truly dreadful. So he started drinking passive-aggressively to get at them since the only way he could communicate was to muck everything up. "OK, I'll show you," he said. "Do you want to see what happens?" He couldn't simply hit it on the head. He is no longer insane. He just keeps refilling.'

Shane's drug use has also decreased since the dark days when junkies overdosed in his apartment. It has also been many years since he overcame the heroin addiction that prompted Sinéad O'Connor to call the cops.

'I went on to medicine, the soup, the garbage,' Shane says. That's what I started on, then I managed to persuade them to put me on morphine, which is an active ingredient in heroin. The ones I'm currently taking are the same as MST [Methadone Substitution Therapy], although they look different. I think I was on five grams of heroin at one point. I wasn't really keeping track. You eventually tire of playing it safe. You might as well take five if you can get four large lines up. I injected whenever I had the chance because it was the best rush. I believe smoking causes drowsiness. I was always doing speedballs, but if I ran out of heroin, the speed kept me going for a while. But if there was heroin nearby, I'd be fucked. You're longing for it.'

Many of his pals have died as a result of alcohol and drugs, yet he has survived it all. One of life's great mysteries is how he is still alive. However, his current consumption levels pale in comparison to those of the past, and given that his father and uncle Billy are both in their 90s, he may have inherited the MacGowan constitution.

'I think he has made compromises,' says Jem Finer. It is feasible to spend a significant amount of time with Shane. He may not be everyone's notion of sobriety, but I would say he is mostly sober and articulate, intelligent, and entertaining... He must have an incredible constitution. I'm not sure what causes that, but I imagine certain people are just extraordinarily powerful and adaptable to any kind of diet, like some strange monster living around a volcanic vent - and can take nutrition from anything!'

Shane listened to friends and fans speak about his knack for songwriting and why his music spoke so clearly to them with profound pride and humility. He returned to The Late Late Show in December 2019 for a special tribute. RTE had cast a broad net to gather together people that would not only demonstrate his tremendous regard as an artist, but also the extraordinary geographical and cultural reach of his songs.

Singers, actresses, and others who have crossed his path spoke with host Ryan Tubridy about their admiration for him. Shane sat between the presenter and Victoria, dressed in a white shirt and a smart navy suit, listening intently and occasionally interjecting when his own memories contradicted theirs. Alcohol Action Ireland was outraged when Studio 4 was transformed into a bar, with customers seated around tables of alcohol. However, the recording environment was one of reverence.

Shane's return to The Late Late Show as a national hero completed the circle for him and the show. In the same studio thirty-four years before, legendary host Gay Byrne accused Shane and The Pogues of tarnishing Irish music. Shane was as amused by the claim as he was by the fact that he was being honoured by so many great Irish performers.

Shane MacGowan's place in Irish music history has long been established. His picture is on the wall of fame at the Irish Rock n Roll Museum Experience in Dublin's Temple Bar, with Luke Kelly, Phil Lynott, and Sinéad O'Connor. Many years before he was honoured with the unique lifetime achievement award at the National Concert Hall, The Pogues' significance in broadening the Irish music legacy and bringing generations around the world to it was recognized.

Shane's centrality in the story of Irish music was highlighted by The Late Late Show's tribute, as was the intrinsic relationship between his songs and those he heard as a child on Raidió Tariffs Éireann and Raidió Na Gaeltachta on travels to Tipperary. The appearance of legendary storyteller and singer Seán Sé on the show proved conclusively that Shane's poetic lyrics have their roots in Irish traditional music. Shane was noticeably moved by the 83-year-old's appearance, characterising him as a "huge hero." Sé was one of the first Irish voices he heard, as well as the best friend of Seán Riada, who was a major influence on Shane's music. Sé stated that being in Shane's company was a "privilege," and he spoke of his contribution to Irish tradition.

'When I was very young... in the early forties, I remember hundreds leaving West Cork to find employment in England,' he remarked. 'Then, later on, when I was singing in venues like the White Hart on Fulham Broadway, I met those individuals, and they played Irish music, but with a twist. The Irish in England, like the Clare and Donegal styles, contributed their own dimension. For example, they made the piano accordion respectable, which had previously been considered taboo.

'Shane has been a hero of mine, and there's one thing that distinguishes him: if someone writes a song that will be performed for as long as there are Irish or Americans on this planet, it's a unique achievement, and that's what "Fairytale Of New York" has done.'

Shane watched in astonishment as Sean sang a piece of 'The Body Of An American' accompanied by a band. Before conducting the song, which was famously featured in the hit US series The Wire, Seán described its opening lines as "a wonderful poem, a requiem for a paddy."

Shane, in contrast to previous appearances on RTE chat shows, was aware and in excellent spirits. He was also eager to perform and was backed by more than a dozen musicians, including The Pogues' Jem Finer and Terry Woods, Steve Wickham, a renowned violin player and Shane's cousin, and Fiachna Braonáin, guitarist with Hothouse Flowers. 'White City' and 'Sally MacLennane' were taken from The Pogues' enormous songbook before seasoned country singer Philomena Begley joined him to sing 'Fairytale Of New York'.

Siobhan remembered their youth in the fireside chat hosted by Tubridy, and Shane spoke, as he had so often, about the influence of his mother's family at the cottage in Tipperary and the music he listened to there. As they did so, a screen displayed black-and-white images from Shane's favourite vacations.

The show not only traced the beginnings of Shane's songs, but also investigated why they became the connective tissue between Irish people living outside Ireland and their musical and cultural heritage. Despite their international fame as a 'Irish band,' The Pogues were a London band, and none of the original six were born in Ireland. Jem was from Stoke-on-Trent, James was from Worsley, Manchester, Andrew was from west London, and Spider was from Eastbourne, Sussex. Shane was the only band member whose parents were both Irish, while Cait was born in Nigeria to an Irish father and a Scottish mother. The trio didn't have any Irish-born musicians until Philip Chevron and Terry Woods joined.

As Seán Sé pointed out, The Pogues' arrival in London rather than Ireland gave them such a ferocious energy and allowed them to add an edgier dimension to Irish traditional music. Their interpretations of classic songs such as 'The Auld Triangle,' 'Waxies Dargle,' 'Poor Paddy,' and 'Kitty' gave the London Irish access to and pride in their cultural history.

Glen Hansard, a songwriter from north Dublin, witnessed firsthand what The Pogues meant to Irish people in London. 'What made Shane's and The Pogues' music unusual for me was that they were speaking to the broad diaspora - and the word diaspora implies the scattered tribe,' he explained on the show. 'I recall seeing The Pogues in London in the late 1980s at the Town & Country Club, and there was a terrible energy in the room. I was terrified because it was mental energy. My cousins in Birmingham used to sing Irish tunes much more enthusiastically than I or my parents ever did. And it had something to do with being away from Ireland, not being entirely English or Irish, and hence leaning into the identity. So when The Pogues appeared, it was like a blast of passion and commitment.'

Far beyond only speaking to the Irish in Britain, The Pogues gave individuals of Irish origin residing in the United States a band to call their own. Martin O'Malley, a former US presidential contender and the governor of Baltimore, met The Pogues on tour in America, and his band, O'Malley's March, backed them up. He flew to Ireland for the special memorial event and spoke passionately about Shane's songs' impact on Irish Americans.

'I have respected this man for so long: his passion, his range,' Martin said. And I'm not talking about the number of notes he sings; I'm talking about the fact that as an Irish American kid growing up in the 1970s and 1980s in the United States, the Clancy Brothers and Tommy Makem were our main portals to an understanding of things Irish through music. It was wonderful, but it was always our parents' music. But when this guy with the emotion and the fierceness came along, it altered everything, and it wasn't just a young kid singing old songs, you know? It was him who made old tunes new again. I'd seen him several times at the 9:30 Club and the Guinness Fleadh in New York. He has done so much for Irish music and Irish music in general throughout the diaspora.'I know a lot of the talk in the UK has been about the Irish, but songs like "The Body Of An American" and other songs - "Thousands Are Sailing" - were a real link for us. That made the song more impassioned, and it became ours. I went to the 9:30 Club, and I remember getting in there late, and there was this mob of young Irish American kids all jumping up and down like sea waves to "Roddy McCorley." "My God, it's all new again," I thought, and our music took a different turn; we added drums and electric guitar.'

Shane's global fan base has always included well-known actors, some of whom have become friends. Aidan Gillen and Patrick Bergin both appeared on The Late Late Show to recognize his contribution, while Tom Vaughan-Lawlor and Liam Neeson sent video messages. 'You took components of Irish culture and music, kicked it in the backside with a huge sense of pride, excitement, and rebellion, and sent it out into the world,' Liam added. 'And that was feckin' amazing, and it stopped us all moping into our pints or Baileys Irish Cream, and we took pride in ourselves,' he says.

Bobby Gillespie taped a tribute, as did Paul Simon, another celebrity enthusiast whose bond with Shane is less well known. 'I'm here to salute my buddy Shane MacGowan, whose voice conveyed something profound and lovely about the Irish soul,' he explained.

Victoria described how Paul became close to Shane after making him an unannounced visit. 'He was in Dublin and asked the driver if he knew Shane MacGowan, and the guy happened to know us,' she explained. "Look, I'd love to meet him," he said. "Can you assist me in meeting him?"

'So the driver called and said, "Look, Paul Simon wants to come around to your house."So he came over and spent the entire day conversing with Shane, playing music, and having a great time, and he said it was the finest day he'd ever had in his life. He realised Shane had a really poor record player, so he sent him a state-of-the-art one, and now he comes and hangs out every time he's here. He's a tremendously kind man and a songwriter's songwriter, so they can chat about music for hours.'

Shane and friends shared memories and sang songs until the early hours of the morning at RTE's after-show celebration. Some of his Nenagh mates, including Noel and Scruffy Kenny, were also present to toast him on his special night.

Shane found solace in The Late Late Show, which received extensive media coverage in Ireland. Victoria told me the next day that she was glad he was so driven to perform: 'I think he will get back on his feet and come back out there and he will be playing.'He wanted more performances, but he also wanted RTE to allow him to sing more songs and give him his own program. He wanted to keep doing it, which shocked me because I expected it would be difficult to get him to do even one song. But, in reality, he wanted to do the entire damned thing. He did not want anyone else to sing. "No, I want to do it all," he said. He was really angry that other individuals were singing. So I believe he has reclaimed that.'

Victoria is hopeful that the creative block that has hindered his creativity for so long will be lifted and he will begin writing new songs. 'I think he's only ever been moving because he's been motivated to write and perform,' she says. 'So, now he's kind of got that back,' she says of the prize he received in 2018. It has just been in the last year, and even in the latter half of this year. I believe the Ivor Novello award played a role. That, I believe, propelled him. He'd certainly dispute it, but I believe he's still motivated by getting that music out there.'

The media revelations of a comeback solo album in March 2020 confirmed this rekindled urge to record new material. According to the Irish Sun, Shane recorded five songs with the help of Johnny and Michael Cronin, as well as fellow band members Fiachra Milner and Brian Murphy. 'Shane has such a beautiful voice,' Johnny Cronin noted. 'He's been blasting through vocal takes and impressing everyone with his intensity. It's a dream come true to be recording with Shane. He's not only fantastic fun, but he has such a presence and so many ideas that they're spilling out of him.'

Restrictions established in the aftermath of the Covid-19 outbreak limited these studio sessions and kept Shane at home for the rest of 2020, with the exception of an appearance on The Late Late Show's traditional Christmas busk for the Simon Community. He sang a touching rendition of 'Raglan Road,' Patrick Kavanagh's poem about the famed tree-lined lane not far from Shane's home in Ballsbridge, alongside John Sheahan, Glen Hansard, Lisa O'Neill, and Finbar Furey.

As the most amazing of years came to an end, the release of the film Crock of Gold: A Few Rounds starring Shane MacGowan thrust him back into the spotlight. It was exhibited in theatres, but was mostly streamed online by fans. It was produced by Johnny Depp and directed by Julien Temple. It's a visual feast that weaves together audio and video material with spectacular animation effects to convey his narrative and investigate what made him who he is. We enter the film through splitting clouds and see a map of Ireland with its ancient legends before being swooped into the farmhouse that sparked Shane's young imagination. 'God looked down on this tiny cottage in Ireland and said, "That little boy there, he's the little boy I'm gonna use to save Irish music and take it to greater popularity than it's ever had before." 'Why would God do that?' Victoria wonders. 'Because God is Irish,' says the reply.

In the opening sequences, cobwebbed religious monuments, the Sacred Heart of Jesus, and film reenacting his boyhood visits to The Commons are used to dramatic effect, evoking the 'old Ireland' in which his lyrics are rooted. The juxtaposition of these sepia-toned scenes with animation and archival interview material gives the film a unique and kaleidoscopic appearance, in line with the subject's restless mind.

However, the director encountered a gigantic obstacle in making the picture. Shane declined to be interviewed, despite the fact that it was Shane's idea and Johnny Depp had to persuade Julien to take on the project. Worse, he was irascible, confrontational, and belligerent towards Julien and the crew at times. 'The essential skill for me was to learn how to let the abuse roll off my back - to literally become a duck,' Julien says. 'It swings from one extreme to another in a way, so you just have to live with it. My biggest worry was collecting people's money and then failing to deliver.'

Several attempts were made to film Shane at home, but none were successful. Infuriated, the director opted to film people with whom Shane felt more at ease conversing in the hopes of drawing him out. This was also difficult. 'We asked all The Pogues, but they didn't want to go near it with a bargepole,' Julien says. So we ended up with this bizarre mix of people that Shane was pleased to speak to, but who were also keen to speak to Shane because convincing people was equally difficult.'

The first time they attempted to film Shane and Johnny Depp together, Johnny failed to appear. The next night, Johnny showed up, but no Shane. When they both appeared on the third try, the eight hours of tape collected gave only a few minutes of usable material. Other friends who attempted to elicit some usable footage had conflicting reactions. Bobby Gillespie's polite inquiry regarding when Shane had gone to England touched a sensitive emotion. He was accused of "interrogating" him and instructed to "change the subject." Shane, on the other hand, was the epitome of courtesy when Gerry Adams paid a visit to his Dublin flat. 'There's no excuse for you not to write more songs,' Gerry said. 'No, you know, I'm doing my best,' Shane answered. 'Are you writing right now?' he inquired. 'I've ran out of ideas right now,' Shane admitted.

This uncommon admission of his difficulty to write was very heartbreaking, especially in light of comments from previous interviews. 'Songs are just floating about in the air,' he used to say. 'That's why tubes are called airs. We only need to reach out and get them. That's why I'm always grabbing, because if I don't reach out and get it, it'll continue on its journey to Paul Simon.'

Julien Temple has no remorse about the way Shane obstructed the making of Crock of Gold, and believes the way the tale was ultimately conveyed benefited it. 'I wanted to depict these several versions of him, this shattered feeling of his paradoxes. These various characters are the source of his creative strength. I wanted to let viewers form their own opinions, to show these several snippets of him recounting the same narrative in dramatically different ways: the untrustworthy narrator is a key element of Shane.

'It doesn't really matter if it's objectively true. It's sometimes more crucial that he believes it's true because it allows him to be himself. He wouldn't be Shane MacGowan if he wasn't permitted to believe things that weren't true, and it's all wrapped up in the mists of Irish mythology, legend, and literature. It's all part of his innate sense of who he's become. But I believe everyone does it to some level.'

Crock of Gold also shed light on a subject that has preoccupied Shane's agitated mind since he was a child: death. On visits to The Commons, he slept in his aunty Nora's bed, and he was 'always scared she'd die in her sleep' due to her chain smoking. He'd developed a sick fascination with the farm's killing of geese and turkeys, as well as how they appeared when they died. He would walk into Therese's room every morning and 'kick her to see whether she was alive' when she was on hefty medicines to calm her anxiety at the Barbican.

One of the causes for his strong Irish Catholic religion was his fear about loss and death, very certainly his own. 'I was reading Marx and Trotsky one day, and I suppose that's when I lost faith,' he explained. 'It hit me like a lightning bolt. I suddenly thought, What if it's a pile of nonsense? And I failed. I tried and tried to rebuild my trust, but you just can't. I converted to atheism. It scared the crap out of me. It meant I'd never see the great elderly people again after they died, and some of them had already passed away.'

Ann Scanlon is a devout Irish Catholic who understands how important Shane's dedication is to him. 'I pray to Mary and Jesus, and Saint Martin and Saint Francis, but I also pray to my deceased relatives who I view as saints,' she explains. That is also true for me. I could only live with my mother's death by knowing that I will see her again one day, and my religion has been the greatest gift in my life to me, and Shane has the same. It was incredibly poignant at the end of his 60th birthday concert when he just raised his glass and exclaimed in Gaelic, "For God and Ireland." Shane, I mean: his country and his faith.'

Many people have taken Shane's hedonistic tendencies as proof of a death wish. Shane, on the other hand, refutes this, and while he may appear fragile for his 63 years, he is still alive - the ultimate survivor. "'If I wanted to die, I'd be dead already," he says in the video, and "I don't see him having a death-wish in any shape or form," Julien Temple says. 'You almost get the impression he's pickled, that he's preserved in some way from the chemicals as long as he maintains a kind of balance on it. He's not drinking to become drunk; rather, he's replenishing a system that maintains him in a happy mood."

It has, of course, come at a high cost. He hasn't walked in nearly five years. His days are spent in a recliner, his gaze fixed on his favourite television. Caregivers help him get in and out of bed. Some of his physical fragility, as seen in Crock of Gold, upsets those who know him. Ann Scanlon, on the other hand, looks past his limitations to the intellectual and thoughtful man she has always known, strengthened by his religion.

'He's had a lot of scrapes over the years and that's his physique, but with Shane, people have always focused on the way he looks, even back in the day,' she says. That is something I never see. Shane is a celestial entity. Gerry [O'Boyle] compares himself to a cross between composer Turlough O'Carolan and Saint Francis, which may seem exaggerated, but I can see it - the Irish Mozart and Saint Francis dealing with mankind. Shane has a feeling of divinity, and his Irish

Catholicism is vitally essential to him; it serves as his spiritual superstructure.'

Shane's reputation as one of Ireland's most gifted writers and performers is well-known around the world. For more than 35 years, he has been an inspirational figure to followers, a legend who made Irish music cool and instilled even more pride in the diaspora. While some of The Pogues' contemporaries posed on luxury yachts and embraced the yuppie attitude, Shane depicted the other side of eighties England, with songs that were visceral and brutal. Characters in his songs puked in church, slept impoverished in doorways, or were plagued by war. The writer who was inspired by old Ireland set to music the stories he'd once written in his schoolbooks. In doing so, he not only ignited a hitherto unthinkable interest in Irish music, but he also transformed how many people regarded Ireland itself. By fusing its rich culture and violent struggles with punk's insurgent spirit, he opened the door to a country many fans had never visited and knew little about.

The prospect of another 'Rainy Night In Soho' or 'Fairytale Of New York' from his pen remains enticing, and fans around the world hope his muse can be rediscovered. When Victoria asks him near the end of Crock of Gold if there's anything he'd like to happen in his life, he says, 'Yes, I'd like to start prolifically writing songs again.' 'And I'd like to be able to play pool,' he adds after a brief pause.

He has a rock of support in Victoria. She, as well as his family and friends, are always encouraging. They understand, however, that any motivation to walk again and write new songs must come from him alone. He, for one, insists on the surgery that would restore his mobility and independence, and his writing pad is never far away. Shane MacGowan is not done yet. He is, after all, a man of extremes, and his 'furious devotion' for life remains as fervent as his love of a drink.

The contents of this book may not be copied, reproduced or transmitted without the express written permission of the author or publisher. Under no circumstances will the publisher or author be responsible or liable for any damages, compensation or monetary loss arising from the information contained in this book, whether directly or indirectly. .

Disclaimer Notice:

Although the author and publisher have made every effort to ensure the accuracy and completeness of the content, they do not, however, make any representations or warranties as to the accuracy, completeness, or reliability of the content. , suitability or availability of the information, products, services or related graphics contained in the book for any purpose. Readers are solely responsible for their use of the information contained in this book

Every effort has been made to make this book possible. If any omission or error has occurred unintentionally, the author and publisher will be happy to acknowledge it in upcoming versions.

Copyright © 2023

All rights reserved.